CN00692489

BOLTON ABBEY

THE YORKSHIRE ESTATE OF THE DUKES OF DEVONSHIRE

John M. Sheard

Copyright © John Michael Sheard

First Published 2007

The right of John Michael Sheard to be identified as the author of this work has been asserted by him in accordance with the Copyright, Design and Patents Act, 1988.

All rights reserved. No part of this publication may be reproduced in any form or by any means electronic or mechanical, photocopying, recording, or by any information storage or retrieval system, including the Intenet, without the permission of the Author or publisher.

ISBN 978-0-9556633-0-7 (Hardback)

Designed, printed and bound by:
The Amadeus Press
Ezra House, West 26 Business Park,
Cleckheaton BD19 4TQ

(Front Cover) *View of Bolton Priory by V K Guy Windermere*

(Back Cover) *The Strid, Bolton Abbey by V K Guy Windermere*

Contents

Bolton Priory by Granville Harris, Leeds

Acknowledgements

Very little appears to have been written about Bolton Abbey except for guidebooks about the Priory and walks along the river Wharfe or to the Strid. However, as many books have now been written about Chatsworth, the main family seat of the Duke and Duchess of Devonshire, I considered that Bolton Abbey would also make a good subject for a book. In a different way, Bolton Abbey, is precious too, and so I started to jot down my thoughts on living and working there, which were the beginnings of this book.

In the course of writing this book I have spoken to many people who have helped me by generously sharing their knowledge, their time and by providing me with invaluable research. I must thank all the people who live on the Estate, tenants, employees and all their families who have created and maintained a beautiful part of Wharfedale, worthy of much enjoyment by others and truly deserving of much recognition.

Although, there is no great house to write about the history and landscape of this part of the Yorkshire Dales makes it truly special. I have much pleasure in listing those who have greatly assisted me by contributing to this book with general knowledge or photographs:

Duke and Duchess of Devonshire

Dowager Duchess of Devonshire

The Trustees of the Chatsworth Settlement

Currey & Co., Solicitors, London

Staff and tenants of the Bolton Abbey Estate 1966 to the present day

Catherine Owens

Sedbergh School Foundation

Country Land and Business Association

Devonshire Arms Country House Hotel

Game Conservancy Trust

Royal Institution of Chartered Surveyors

Yorkshire Dales National Park

Yorkshire Dales Millennium Trust

English Nature

English Heritage

Forestry Commission and Authority

Yorkshire Dales Society

Department of Environmental Food and Rural Affairs

Staff at the Farmers Guardian and Country View

Yorkshire Tourist Board

The Royal Agricultural College, Cirencester

Wharfedale Naturalists Society

Owl Project, Muncaster, Cumbria

Craven Herald and Pioneer

Ordnance Survey

Ash Marketing, Ilkley

Yorventure

Foreword

By The Dowager Duchess of Devonshire

It is a pleasure for me to have been asked to write a foreword to this memoir. Reading it has taken me back over the years and reminded me of John's life and work as resident land agent, a profession becoming ever rarer as estates are broken up or the landowner turns to a firm that works on other estates and employs specialists in each department – farms, forestry etc.

A resident agent is always on duty and has to be a jack of all trades ready to deal with everything that can happen in rural England, including legal and technical matters. John was responsible for the well-being of the tenants of formerly 85 but now 52 farms, their farmhouses and buildings, the workforce employed directly by him, including the game keepers who looked after one of the best grouse moors in England and several miles of fishing on the river Wharfe, quarries, let houses and 85 miles of footpaths through some of the most spectacular country in England.

Visitors return again and again to enjoy this very English place. The dramatic sight of the Priory Church, the Rectory, the Boyle Room and Bolton Hall grouped near the river Wharfe make an unforgettable impression when approached through the Hole in the Wall high above the west bank of the river. The latter makes its own rules and changes its face almost daily.

During John's years as agent the expectations of tenants and visitors (who make a vital contribution to the Estate through car parking fees) have changed profoundly and more must be provided for them. For the residents of the village and the scattered farms a new Village Hall has been built, the Devonshire Arms Hotel was taken in hand and greatly enlarged by the Trustees, but the biggest plus of all was that my son and daughter-in-law lived in Beamsley Hall, so Bolton Abbey was home to their children.

The grouse moor covers half the acreage of the Estate and is famous in the sporting world. Its management is a law unto itself. John oversaw the new access agreements to the moors, which allow more freedom for walkers and led the way for other landowners to follow.

Among the ancient buildings on the Estate is Barden Tower and John clarifies the complicated story of Lady Anne Clifford's (1590-1676) long negotiations to stake her claim for its ownership.

For my family and myself this book is a fascinating record of John's 33 year stewardship, professionally, quietly and sympathetically carried out. Andrew and his Trustees had complete confidence in him and his staff.

Andrew and his brother Billy enjoyed the August visits of the family since early childhood, when the Cavendish children and their cousins were boarded

11th Duke and Duchess of Devonshire

Reproduced by permissin of the Chatsworth Settlement Trustees from the Devonshire Collection, Chatsworth

out in farmhouses and the Post Office as Bolton Hall was full up with his grandfather's shooting guests. After we were married and the war was over our annual visits bound us to Bolton Abbey with deep affection. A holiday atmosphere greeted us, which was looked forward to with pleasure all year and never disappointed.

John was instrumental in all of this. Andrew would have agreed with all I have tried to say, but he would have said it better. No one appreciated John's loyal service more than he did.

I recommend this book to anyone familiar with life on a country estate, who will find much to interest them in the diverse happenings of its day to day running. To those who have no knowledge of such a job it explains the role of the agent.

There were only three agents in 113 years from 1885 to 1998. John succeeded two remarkable holders of the office and made his own mark from which all have benefited.

Deborah Devonshire

Preface

Bolton Priory and Stepping Stones across the River Wharfe

The Bolton Abbey Estate has been owned, managed and developed over the years by the Dukes of Devonshire since their inheritance in 1755, and it has been customary for the management to be under the care of a Resident Land Agent. I was delighted to be appointed to such a post in 1966, and to work with Andrew Cavendish, the 11th Duke of Devonshire. Both he, and the Duchess have taken a great personal interest in the management of Bolton Abbey, and particularly in its tenants and the people involved with its care and development.

My stewardship extended until retirement in July 1998 and this book gives an overview of the many interests at Bolton Abbey and describes briefly how the Estate was run. I could not have worked for a more devoted and generous person whose whole family became interested in the welfare of the Estate.

The Dukes of Devonshire have been at the centre of

Bolton Priory as perceived by J.M.W. Turner 1775-1851

Copyright: The Trustees of the British Museum

English political and cultural life for more than four centuries. Individually they have led in the worlds of politics, science and the arts. Although the 11th Duke being the second son of the 10th Duke of Devonshire never really expected to be a duke his contribution to the arts, politics and the preservation of their country estates in England and Ireland was outstanding. Andrew Cavendish inherited the title because sadly his elder brother was killed in action towards the end of the Second World War. During the War he also saw active service and was awarded the Military Cross for leading his company to capture and hold a hill during the Italian Campaign, whilst under fire and with dwindling supplies.

His father died early, aged only 55, and Andrew became the 11th Duke of Devonshire at just 30 years of age. Unfortunately, he inherited enormous death duties but despite considerable financial pressure the Duke ensured the Bolton Abbey Estate remained largely intact. A keen art collector, sportsman and politician he was also a pioneer, bridging the gap between the age-old aristocracy and today's egalitarian society. The Duke was reported to have said that everyone "was welcome in my back garden".

He encouraged the public to enjoy the whole of the Bolton Abbey Estate in Wharfedale by investing in

Andrew Cavendish 11th Duke of Devonshire KG, MC 1920-2004

Reproduced by permission of the Chatsworth Settlement Trustees

visitor facilities and conserving the landscape's natural charm. This hopefully will ensure its future as a place of tranquillity and beauty for generations to come.

The Devonshire family have always hoped that the Estate is of as much interest to all its visitors, as it is to them. They wish to maintain and keep it as a worthwhile place in which to live and work, and to enjoy some of the best countryside in the Yorkshire Dales.

It was a great sadness when the 11th Duke died on 3rd May 2004 at the age of 84, having had 54 years tenure, but he will be remembered by many with great affection both as a "popular aristocrat whose life was spent struggling with his inheritance", as a generous friend and quintessential English gentleman.

His son, the Marquess of Hartington, who came to live on the Bolton Abbey Estate in 1982 succeeded him. I am eternally grateful for the encouragement and support received from the late Duke and the current Duke and their families.

The diverse nature of the Estate has evolved over many centuries with the moorlands, woodlands, River Wharfe and farming activities creating this unique landscape.

The Estate has a long history of maintaining, preserving and enhancing this part of Wharfedale for multiple objectives, and great emphasis has been placed upon its many features of natural and historic interests.

When considering the purpose of this book and reflecting on my past education and work, I realised what an enormous contribution my schooling had made to my ability to enjoy my career and life at Bolton Abbey. For this reason, I would like all the proceeds earned from this book to go to students at Sedbergh School, Cumbria. I was educated there from 1948 to 1953, and am extremely grateful for the way it prepared me for living in the modern world, as well as providing an outstanding appreciation of country surroundings.

All profits from the sale of this book will, through the Sedbergh School Foundation Registered Charity No. 529904 help students particularly those from Yorkshire who may need financial support in order to complete or extend their studies. For myself, I hope that they will enjoy full lives that allow them to use their talents for the benefit of others.

John M. Sheard, 2006

INTRODUCTION

What is available to the general public now at Bolton Abbey has been made possible by the landowners, the Dukes of Devonshire, and particularly the increased access by the 11th Duke.

There is a feeling of calm which is inherit amongst this ancient Estate in spite of it becoming one of Yorkshire's visitor attractions. It may be the history of its ancient buildings, or the space of grassland, the river or woodland scenery, but there is an awareness that all is protected and has been for several generations.

The most famous of the spectacular ruins is the old Priory lying beside the river Wharfe, and thousands of people approach through the 'hole in the wall'. This can lead to short or long magnificent walks along the riverside, and reaching the Strid, where at its narrowest point it is only three metres wide.

Happily the nave of the Priory was saved from destruction in 1539 by a concession of Henry VIII, and survives today as a well supported and active parish church.

A bench seat has been placed around the tree on the village green to commemorate the 21st birthday of the 11th Duke's grandson, the Earl of Burlington. Another wooden seat has been constructed and placed in the village with a stunning view of the Priory and river commemorating the 11th Duke and Duchess's golden wedding anniversary.

There is a strong community bond amongst the people who live in the village because most either work on the Estate or are retired employees. Even when the new village shop was built in the late 1990s, it had to blend naturally with the other buildings and, to conform to timelessness, an old red post box and red telephone box were positioned outside. The building is also a visitor centre providing a means of welcome to all visitors, information on the Estate and detailed leaflets explaining walks, natural wildlife etc.

The Pantry shop, opened in 2002 is a good example of the Estate's policy to contribute help to both residents and visitors for it has available both bread and locally baked items as well as frozen foods and luxury items perhaps more attractive to the visitors.

The 6th Duke of Devonshire granted public access to the Strid and to some of the riverside but in the late 1800s a new railway station was built at Bolton Abbey, which probably established a tourist phenomenon particularly at weekends. But the 11th Duke granted Open Access on the moors and created 85 miles of footpaths available to the public which certainly established major interest for people who enjoy the countryside, farming, woodlands, wildlife, heather moorlands or merely just picnicking along the riverside.

He has been able to accommodate and accept public interest whilst maintaining his own family interest and responsibilities in a way which hopefully will be acceptable for many years.

The Duke and Duchess on their Golden Wedding Anniversary seat

I had always understood that managing an Estate is a professional business and comprehensive knowledge of:- property law, surveying, farming, forestry, minerals, quarrying, field sports, building construction, rights of way both private and public, game laws, law of the land, employment etc., amongst a host of other subjects.

What I had not realised was how much time would be spent dealing with people, the office routine and balancing one person's needs against another's. Trying to understand what individuals really want, and why do some urbanites drive endless miles to have a picnic in the country and are so often seen on a roadside verge eating sandwiches coated in exhaust fumes.

Understanding people at all levels of their professions or activities is so important when accepting responsibility for managing large acreages of part of the British landscape on behalf of the owner. As there are so many interests enjoyed by members of the public; professional, amenity, wildlife, physical exercise, history, heritage objects, photography, artistic paintings and of course RAMBLING, and many more interests so whether the public bring enquiries or complaints you need to know immediately by asking '…and what is your interest?'

Expect to be amazed, for that is what makes life in the country so enormously interesting, and that brings you face to face with reality by learning the ever changing interests of people, thankfully most are friendly.

John M Sheard

THE ESTATE HAS A VARIETY OF BUILDINGS

The Estate is as rich in the variety of its buildings as it is in the diversity of its landscape, each worthy of careful note as one passes through the villages. They become even more absorbing as one wanders the footpaths and discovers the history and lifestyles that previous generations brought to Wharfedale.

Most people arrive by car in today's instant society, but in earlier generations different factors influenced the building of the Estate, none more so than the Augustinian Canons who settled in the lower meadows adjoining the banks of the Wharfe and decided that building their Priory here must be the most beautiful place outside heaven with all the natural resources to set down their roots with water from the springs on the hillside adjacent to the Gatehouse (which now forms the dining hall at Bolton Hall) for their food and beer. Furthermore

Stone Arch, formerly the aqueduct at Bolton Abbey

they were blessed with an abundance of water from the surrounding hills that was directed into a man made water course or "leat" with a gentle gradient to power the overshot waterwheel which graced the south gable of the Corn Mill at Bolton Abbey. Many will have seen the building and perhaps been mystified by the three arch stone structure astride the B6160 road built as an aqueduct to feed the waterwheel.

A few strides away there remains the original ice house – for generations this was the local freezer for the Duke's pantry.

Bolton Hall has its own history which is beyond the scope of this book, however the building department has maintained the Hall for over 250 years of the Duke's ownership under guidance of the Clerks of Work, who were historically appointed by the King or Duke of the realm to build their castles, fortified houses and buildings of importance. They had the power to second any material or craftsmen to undertake this work and those refusing faced the risk of imprisonment.

Today the position is more congenial, although it is still the responsibility to advise on repairs, alterations, extensions or development of many properties forming the Estate's built environment.

Most properties are built from local gritstones that can be seen from rock escarpments along the valley hillsides. Canons employed and taught stonemasonry, carpentry, leadwork and carving skills, although it was not uncommon for good craftsmen to travel and lodge where work was in abundance

The Tithe Barn at Bolton Abbey

and well paid. Indeed there are many links researched by archaeologists and conservationists that have identified craftsmen's marks used on the Priory and the Tithe Barn (or Great Barn).

The Tithe Barn is a unique building and remains one of the largest double aisled barns in the country. The timbers are of immense proportions of solid English oak grown within the sight of the building. There are still remnants of these huge trees in the Laund Pastures.

The Estate was rich in wool and produced sufficient to attract merchants from as far away as Italy to buy the whole annual crop stored in the Tithe Barn. This in turn influenced the building of farms in the landscape to share in this new found wealth.

Today's farms are a lasting legacy to the families who shaped and tilled the land over generations enduring both feast and hardship. Each one has its own historic character. Inglenook fireplaces are not uncommon, as are cottages with beehive ovens, cruck barns and remnants of heather or ling thatch, dry walled barns, water wells, lime kilns and bridges are a whole host of examples where the land has given of its wealth and provided all the materials necessary to support life in the dale.

In recent years we have been fortunate to invest the Estate's income in renovating buildings and in some instances even providing new buildings.

There is much interest today in energy conservation, recycling carbon emissions and re-use of existing materials. In the last twenty years as many as 50 roofs have been renovated through removal of the existing slates, repairing the woodwork before re-fixing the existing slates on new underfelt and laths. An alternative to stone slates can be seen in the dark grey Burlington Slate from the Cumbrian

The old and new Forge garage at Bolton Abbey

mountains, probably due to a lack of availability of the stone slates as is the case today. Most current building renovation and extensions re-use stone from redundant buildings scattered in the landscape or from old farm steadings.

The Forge Garage built in 1997 replaced an early 1920s building attached to the Abbey Tea Rooms, where the original door to the forge still hangs at the entrance with the local farmers branding iron marks scorched into the woodwork from the Wood family's smithy in its early days.

The Abbey Tea Rooms is a splendid example of the recycling of a redundant building into alternative use, retaining much of its original character at a reasonable cost and now giving pleasure to many visitors plus employment for local people.

The Pantry (completed in 2002) on the Village Green was for many years the Clerk of Works office, previously it was the original Estate Office when the whole Estate was possibly managed by four people (the Duke's appointed agent, Clerk of Works, Head Game Keeper and Head Forester). Escalation of administration has instigated the necessary expansion of all aspects of management, and in the year 2000 it was decided to integrate all the satellite offices that had mushroomed around the village into a larger Estate Office designed and built from the Estate's resources into an award winning building.

In the late 1990s a similar exercise was undertaken – taking into account congestion in the Village Shop, the dilapidation of the information trailer and the isolation of the ice-cream kiosk. With the Trustees approval a new Village Shop and Information Centre was built and has become the focal point for people to browse and buy their gifts and refreshments.

The Cavendish Pavilion, renovated in 1992, is perhaps one of the most unique buildings in the

The Cavendish Pavilion 1901 at Sandholme Car Park

Inset: The Pantry Shop in Bolton Abbey

National Park and unlike any other you are likely to see. It was built in 1901 to provide a refreshment centre for the thousands of weekend visitors arriving from the new railway line into Bolton Abbey. One theory of origin is that the Duke's agent would have had a close liaison with the Railway's agent and perhaps mentioned that he needed a new refreshment building for his visitors… "well why not talk to the people who are building the new station" the building erected was timber framed with a concrete floor, corrugated metal roof and a wonderful cast iron external urinal to the rear – all very typical of the rural railway station architecture found at places like Hellifield.

Many of the dwellings had been starved of investment due to the heavy payment of death duties and in recent years there has been an opportunity to renovate many of the houses, manor halls, cottages and farms in order to secure their future for the next generations.

Work continues and more recently a new information centre at Strid Wood was completed in 2005 after much consultation and a final blessing from the Duchess of Devonshire ensuring the long term benefit of an interesting design in this beautiful part of Wharfedale.

There is a wealth of historic and interesting buildings always requiring careful attention that will in the future become an inheritance for the next generation and the interest of their visitors.

Leslie Gore (Chief Clerk of Works)

A Medieval Estate Surviving

A large agricultural estate was formed at Bolton Abbey in the 12th century when the Augustinian Canons arrived in 1154 and started to build a priory. The land was given to them by Lady Alice de Romille of Skipton Castle for as she put it, "the well being of my soul and those of my forebears and descendents". The valley was fertile with rich land along the sides of the River Wharfe, well grown trees and shrubs along the hillsides, and much heather on the high land forming extensive areas of rough grazing and moorland.

The Canons were interested in establishing a Priory with a devout religious routine, but this land provided them with interesting possibilities for commercial development. In addition to their unremitting rounds of prayer and worship, they also preached, taught, ran hospitals, gave shelter to travellers and ministered as priests. Their main income came from farming operations, tithes, sales of wool and also rents, mills, lead mines and other enterprises. They were soon involved in extensive farming focussing on the breeding of sheep which enabled them to take advantage of the flourishing wool trade.

Monasteries were active in lead mining, metal working, horse breeding, bee keeping, cheese making, and other activities, but wool production was the most profitable. Like Fountains Abbey they exported wool to Flanders and Italy. Monasteries became crucial to the economy of the country and the social well being of the Dales. Their huge upland sheep ranches were managed from farms called Granges. The wool trade created enormous wealth, and the Canons used the revenue to build corn mills, roads and bridges across the river. However, life was not all a bed of roses as the Estate was raided from time to time by the Scots, and finally in 1539 Henry VIII took control of the Priory as part of his Dissolution of the Monasteries.

The Priory was totally closed down with the exception of the nave, and as such ceased to exist, but Henry VIII sold all the land and premises to Henry Clifford, 1st Earl of Cumberland, who lived locally at Skipton Castle. 'Henry Clifford's property eventually passed to the Boyle family and when Charlotte Elizabeth Boyle, became the heiress, she married William Cavendish, who became the 4th Duke of Devonshire in 1755. Lady Charlotte made a good match by marrying the 4th Duke, whose family could be traced back to Bess of Hardwick. However, she certainly could not be accused of marrying for money as she brought several substantial properties and their contents into the family. Burlington House, Bolton Abbey, Chiswick Villa, Londesborough Hall and Lismore Castle were all added to the Cavendish Estates in due course after this marriage, and 250 years later two are thankfully still in the ownership of the Devonshire family. Sadly, Lady Charlotte died at the young age of 23 having had 4 children. Her husband the 4th Duke of Devonshire (1720-1764) was only thirty four on accession, but by chance was

"Bolton Abbey in the Olden Time" by Sir Edwin Landseer 1834
The original hangs at Chatsworth

Copyright: The Trustees of the Chatsworth Settlement

Photography by Sycamore Studios, Skipton

the grandest and richest of the Dukes of Devonshire to date, owning ten great houses, and four immense Estates. He was known for being "universally respected", had great political ability, considerable intelligence and taste and reached what seemed an unassailable position in society and politics.

He became known as the "Crown Prince of the Whigs" and being well supported spent a great deal of time in government, latterly holding office as Prime Minister and then as Lord Chamberlain. However through eventual turmoil in government with men like William Pitt and the Duke of

Newcastle opposed to his views, he resigned his position in 1762.

Sadly his health deteriorated, probably assisted by his service in government and the Great Whig Settlement in politics being destroyed, and died from a stroke in 1764.[1]

His son, William, married Lady Georgiana Spencer who became famous for her charm, intellect, huge gambling debts and enormous hats.

The Estate today consists of remnants of what was a much larger medieval estate. The atmosphere of welcome and peace which is characteristic of Bolton Abbey, comes, I believe, from the fact that this land has been in the very long ownership of one family, and their instinctive understanding of this place. Historians have suggested that the Estate we now see was really created by the Dukes of Devonshire. Their "Cavendish Machine" swung into action and with the encouragement of the Enclosure Awards the land was divided into over 80 small farms, with large areas of land being enclosed and planted as woodland. The Dukes were keen sportsmen and employed keepers to enhance grouse on the moorlands, and fishing on the River Wharfe. The old gatehouse into the Priory precinct was also altered to provide a residence for the Duke.

Left: Charlotte Elizabeth Boyle

Right: William Cavendish 4th Duke of Devonshire

Both the Devonshire Collection

William Spencer Cavendish. 6th Duke of Devonshire (1790-1858)

Portrait by Sir George Hayter (1792-1871)

Approved by the Devonshire Collection

Although, the Dukes of Devonshire live at Chatsworth in Derbyshire, the Bolton Abbey Estate which is largely made up of marginal land and moorland, occupies a special place in the heart of the family. It may not have a grand house, but the landscape of this Yorkshire Dales estate certainly rivals anything that Chatsworth can offer, and, of course, it boasts far better grouse. For well over a century, the name Bolton Abbey has been synonymous with grouse, and every August the Dukes have come and enjoyed the shoot. Bolton Abbey, is a reminder that the interests of the Dukes of Devonshire do spread far beyond the immediate surroundings of their principal seat.

'The 6th Duke of Devonshire (1790-1858) inherited the accession at 21 years of age. He possessed great charm, kindness, considerable taste, a sense of fun and a sensible sense of duty. He inherited such wealth, magnificent possessions and a position in society thought to be second only the to the Royal family's.[2]

'At Chatsworth, amongst his many achievements, the 6th Duke appointed a twenty three year old gardener, who had been in charge of creepers and new plants at the Royal Horticultural Society's garden at Chiswick, to be his Head Gardener. He was called Joseph Paxton and described as a man of "daemonic energy". The first day at Chatsworth he arrived at 4.30 am and recalled the event as follows:- "As no person was to be seen at that early hour I got over the greenhouse gate by the old covered way, explored the pleasure grounds, and looked round the outside of the house. I then went down to the kitchen gardens, scaled the outside wall and saw the whole of the place, set the men to work there at six o'clock, then returned to Chatsworth, and got Thomas Weldon to play me the waterworks and afterwards went to breakfast with poor dear Mrs Gregory and her niece. The latter fell in love with me and I with her, and this completed my first morning's work at Chatsworth before nine o'clock".[3]

The 6th Duke was a bachelor, an avid traveller and collector of works of art which he bought on his European tours. He inherited 8 houses, 200,000 acres of land, and he spent most of his life extending his properties and keeping his estates in good order. In the end his extravagance forced him to sell the Londesborough Estate in order to pay his debts. However, he enhanced much of the Bolton Abbey Estate with the assistance and blessing of his agent, Reverend William Carr who was also the incumbent at Bolton Priory and the second largest agricultural tenant on the Estate. A distinctive waterfall was constructed beside the stepping stones across the river below the Priory; a carriage way and footpaths with stone and timber built shelters were installed in the Strid Wood.

'The 7th Duke (1808-1891) was a keen agriculturalist and a founder member of the Royal Agricultural Society being its president at one stage, but living at Holker Hall in Cumbria his main interest was the formation and development of the Iron and Steel Institute in Barrow, and a huge industry followed founded on iron. Income from Barrow grew from £14,000 in 1863 to £169,000 in 1864. In fact 80% of the Duke's investments centered in Barrow. He was a great Victorian nobleman, moral, intelligent, responsible, wise and also acquired the name of "The Second Iron Duke".

He also sponsored the building and all its apparatus of a laboratory of Experimental Science at Cambridge University which became known as the Cavendish Laboratory. Opened in 1874 and with twenty-two Nobel Prize Awards to 'Cavendish'men it has become the most famous physical laboratory in the world.'[4]

At Bolton Abbey in the lifetime of the 7th Duke a main railway line and station were brought to Bolton Abbey in 1888. When the railway reached Bolton Abbey special trains, even from Sheffield, brought day trippers in their hundreds. Their descendants still come nowadays, walking the paths first created by William Carr. In the lifetime of the 8th Duke in1901 the Cavendish Pavilion was built beside the river to provide refreshment for visitors. Wagonettes were allowed to drive up to the Strid in Strid Wood, and admission tickets were sold to those who wanted to walk on the moorlands or beside the river. The 6th, 7th and 8th Dukes certainly encouraged visitor access to the estate and provided all the main facilities they needed to enjoy their visit. The railway brought thousands of people to the Estate at the weekends, and a new form of tourism was born.

There does not appear to be much recorded at Bolton Abbey by the 8th Duke (1833-1908), but he had spent much of his life as Lord Hartington in distinguished politics where he held great offices of state, and three times had been invited to be the Prime Minister, but three times he refused. 'He was however the only Duke ever to have worn a beard, and was affectionately nicknamed "Harty-Tarty".

He had the habit occasionally of falling asleep in the House of Lords, and on one occasion when he did so he recalled - "and dreamt I was addressing that just assembly, and when someone woke me up I found that my dream was true. I was speaking to their Lordships."

He was known to be "safe" in politics and elsewhere

Barden Tower and Priest House painting by Herbert Royle 1870-1958

Copyright researched

and although at Chatsworth and Bolton Abbey there was some of the best shooting in the country he never boasted of the fact and pretended to be a most indifferent shot. But once he surprised his friends by killing a very high flying partridge with a perfect shot. Everyone cheered, but when the drive was over he asked "I wonder why you all cheered when I fired both barrels at a cock pheasant and missed?" Someone answered that he had killed the highest flying partridge of the day. "Did I?" he replied, "I didn't even know it was there". That spot was immediately named the "Hartington's Stand".

He also had a great passion for the turf, and the Prime Minister, Lord Salisbury, often moaned quietly about the postponement of important parliamentary business because "Devonshire" was obliged to go to Newmarket. But as a steward of the Jockey Club and a fixture in the stand at every classic race, his amiable ill clad presence was immensely popular, and in public his inconsequential shabbiness was something of a trademark. It was perhaps a sign of inverted superiority for he must have known only the heir to the Dukedom could have got away at times with dressing so badly.'[5]

'The 9th Duke, (1868-1938) some thought, being so different from Harty-Tarty, by comparison, was what the middle class democracy thought a Duke should be – the epitomy of a decent, rather dull, typical well-to-do Edwardian, with six children and a dominating wife.

King George V and the Duke of Devonshire at Bolton Abbey railway station

Approved by the Devonshire Collection Chatsworth

Two-thirds of his income was now coming from investments and the political powers were coming less from the ownership of inherited land. However he had considerable experience in politics and was very active in the House of Lords. In 1916 the King appointed him to be the Governor-General of Canada and his wife continued as Mistress of the Robes for the Queen. He settled, complete with five daughters in his family in Ottawa, but was kept very busy. His status was closer to that of the Viceroy of India, dealing directly with the Prime Minister and all war communications between Canada and Britain passed through his office. He was immensely conscientious, but travelled widely, with his family and was always happy when meeting agriculturalists in various parts of the Dominion. The farmers of Canada soon realised he understood their industry.

The Duke and Duchess had a pleasant surprise when a young man, Captain Harold Macmillan, who came to live with them as a new aide-de-camp not only became accepted by the family but eventually married Lady Dorothy their third daughter.

The Duke had a very distinguished career and was admired by all, but sadly, a stroke caused a permanent illness. He maintained the Christmas Parties at Chatsworth which included all his family, parents, children, and his grandchildren, gentry, and all his staff and their guests, reaching 300 or so all provided with wonderful food and dancing into the early hours of the morning. Then all the staff received their Christmas presents. The whole house was full and in spite of all the hard work, the staff felt part of it and loved it. This sort of "nobless oblige" from members of the family was particularly appreciated by the Chatsworth staff."[6]

The 10th Duke (1895-1950) succeeded at the age of 43 years in 1938 and was an accomplished botanical painter. He was particularly interested in politics and that took most of his time and attention. Death duties on his father's demise had been affordable but over time the government now increased the percentage to be paid on the full value of landed Estates, works of art, all valuable assets and he was determined, with the help of his legal advisors, Currey & Co., to make plans for the protection of the family's inheritance. He applied all of his financial ingenuity, and the Chatsworth Estate Company was totally transformed into a Discretionary Trust named the Chatsworth Settlement. After this he was fond of saying that all he possessed were the extremely ancient clothes he stood up in. But he had to live three years and that did not seem a problem. Then the government increased the waiting time to five years, and the rate of duty to 80%. Suddenly and quite unexpectedly while chopping wood at his house, Compton Place, in 1950 he suffered a severe heart attack and died within two hours. Sadly this meant that at his age of 55 years he had died just fourteen weeks too early to avoid the Death Duties. Various properties, landed Estates, and works of art had to be sold, the process taking 24 years but most of Chatsworth, Bolton Abbey, Lismore, Eastbourne and some treasures survived, probably due to the 11th Duke being aided by Mr. Burrows of Currey & Co.

The 11th Duke of Devonshire (1920-2004) inherited the dukedom in 1950, and vividly remembered his first recollection of Bolton Abbey, a place of matchless beauty in 1926. King George V was the guest of his grandfather, for the opening of the season's grouse shooting. As a precocious six year old he was allowed to tell the king on his return from the moors that England cricketers had regained the Ashes. Although living in Derbyshire, he greatly enjoyed his ownership of this Yorkshire Estate, and made many friends among the local people. As he said in an interview shortly before his death, "The Estate, which has been in my family since the 1750s provides over 80 miles of footpaths through some of the most spectacular scenery in England. Whether you wander by the River Wharfe, cross the exposed purple heights of heather moorland, or simply relax and just enjoy being there, I hope that you will gain as much pleasure from Bolton Abbey as has my family over the years". His family motto "Cavendo tutus" (safe with caution) has been followed faithfully over the years, and any changes made to the Estate have been generous and harmonious. He was instrumental in the movement to grant open access to the public on the moorland areas in 1968, to modernise the Estate farms and residential property, and to carry out substantial repair and conservation work to the ruins of Bolton Priory and Barden Tower.

Although, because of the number of visitors it receives, there must be a type of commercial management now, Bolton Abbey still retains its ancient and traditional atmosphere. New buildings like the Village Shop, and Village Hall have joined the old existing ones to cater for the expanding needs of tourism and the growth of community activities, but the 16th century barn in the village has been converted into a small café/restaurant – the Tea Cottage – and has kept its medieval structure.

The Estate has kept a significant impact on rural life and works hard to protect and enhance the employee's and tenant's way of life. On a day-to-day basis the Estate must maintain the sensitive balance between the needs of local people to lead their lives, with the desire that large numbers of visitors now have to share this wonderful place. For this reason, visitor management has an important part to play in the overall strategic planning for the future of the Estate.

In 1954 almost the whole of the Bolton Abbey Estate was incorporated into the newly formed Yorkshire Dales National Park. Today, the Estate extends from just south of Bolton Bridge on the A59 Skipton to Harrogate road, northwards to just before Burnsall on the B6160; its eastern boundary lies near the edge of Thruscoss Reservoir, and on the western side at Rylstone. It covers an area of approximately 52 square miles of Wharfedale which is made up of heather moorland, woodland, hill farms and property in the parishes of Bolton Abbey, Barden, Hazelwood with Storiths, Beamsley, Halton East, Embsay with Eastby, Rylstone, Cracoe, Burnsall, Skyreholme, Thruscross and a small part of Addingham.

Overall, the Estate comprises 30,000 acres (12,120

hectares) of land in Wharfedale, of which 15,000 acres (6,060 hectares) are heather moorland, 1535 acres (620 hectares) are woodland, and the remainder is farm land. The upland areas of the Estate are underlaid by millstone grit which has cliffs and outcrops rising to a height of 485 metres. There are two reservoirs which are leased by Yorkshire Water Services Ltd. on Barden Moor. On the eastern side of the River Wharfe, some fast flowing streams have cut deep gills into the bedrock creating valleys and some crags appear most prominently on the skyline at Simon's Seat, a bold and prominent cluster of rocks at the highest point towering over the valley beneath. The moor rises to 449 metres here, and is within the Yorkshire Dales National Park close to its southern boundary. The gills form some of the most attractive scenery on the Estate, the most well known of which is the popular walkers destination, the Valley of Desolation, which has a spectacular waterfall.

Soils on the moorlands are mainly peat varying in depth, but the natural loam over farmland is more fertile and also over limestone or where glacial deposits have been laid in the valley. Some of the best agricultural land is beside the river and has been ploughed for cereal crops in former years, but now provides good meadows or pasture and fine deciduous tree parkland.

The Estate now has 52 farms which are let to tenants and 144 cottages or houses. 42 houses are "listed" for heritage reasons. Commercial interests for example are: the Devonshire Arms Country House Hotel, the Devonshire Fell Hotel at Burnsall, the Cavendish Pavilion, the Tea Cottage, the Bolton Abbey Café, the Village Shop including the Post Office, the Grove Rare Books Shop, Barden Chapel Crafts, Barden Priest's House, Barden Tower Bunk Barn, Information and Craft shop at Sandholme, Forge Garage, Bolton Abbey Caravan Site, Beamsley Caravan Site, mining, woodlands and sporting interests.

In recent years, it has been of enormous importance to the development of the Estate, that the11th Duke's son, the Marquess of Hartington, and his family chose to live at Bolton Abbey. The Marquess moved to Yorkshire in 1982 and this was a clear demonstration to the community that this place still exerts a strong hold over the affections of the Devonshire family.

It has been said there are few more glorious sights in England's greatest county than the magnificent splendour of Bolton Abbey. If you picked Bolton Abbey as the "jewel in the crown" among Yorkshire's many landscapes for its aristocratic and ancient estate with its river, ruined priory and its 85 miles of country walks you would not be alone in your choice. This place has been admired in the past by artists such as Girtin, Cotman, JMW Turner, Ruskin and Royle, as well as poets like the Brontes and Wordsworth. Their enthusiasm for Bolton Abbey is carried on today by the many artists from all over the world who come to this part of Yorkshire to paint this special landscape.

As it has been traditional for the Duke and Duchess of Devonshire to live in Derbyshire they are not resident at Bolton Abbey for long periods of time but happily the Marquess of Hartington had lived on the Estate for 22 years. For this reason, they have come to rely on the Land Agent and his staff to ensure that the Estate runs smoothly. The Devonshire family's affection for Bolton Abbey and their desire to maintain its special surroundings is at the heart of how these professional managers maintain this beautiful place. It is of considerable importance to the Devonshire family that they continue to conserve, maintain and enhance Bolton Abbey for those who live and work there, the visitors who come to enjoy a day in the country, and for future generations to discover in their turn. Bolton Abbey has to succeed in that most difficult of balancing acts – keeping up as a traditional country Estate and at the same time welcoming visitors.

NOTES

All information from Stags and Serpents by John Pearson 1983

1 P. 70-72
2 P. 116
3 P. 132
4 P. 154
5 P 160-161
6 P 176,178,180,182,190

Managing Change in the Country

Riddings Farm Bolton Abbey and Barden Fell in August

The day-to-day management of an established country estate is a complex undertaking and is usually placed in the hands of persons professionally qualified. Before the 1970s this rural position was held by those who were members of the Chartered Land Agents Society.

Traditionally, Chartered Land Agents were engaged as resident agents on large estates – and their entire employment was with the one estate owner. They were important employees as they were able to advise the owner on legal and technical matters that applied to the estates, and were often totally responsible for their day-to-day running.

However, in the 1970s there was a change in the way Land Agents were trained as the Chartered Land Agents Society amalgamated with the Royal Institution of Chartered Surveyors and so a new broader based qualification was introduced. At the same time specialist firms were set up that took over the management of smaller estates on behalf of several landowners, because, significantly the enforcement of death duties had caused a decline in the number of large country estates in this country. On the surviving larger estates, the traditional practice of training land agents on the job continued. So it was possible for a young person to work on an estate and be trained by the appointed

Land Agent, take professional examinations in due course, and after practical work experience on a farm or with a firm become qualified. In many cases, this young person succeeded his tutor agent and would spend the rest of his working life on the estate. So, Land Agents working in a traditional setting were finding themselves responsible for training and ensuring the recruitment of their successor. At Bolton Abbey Alfred Downs was the resident agent from 1885 retiring in 1937 with 52 years service, and was succeeded by his pupil, Ernest Hey who worked on the Estate for over 40 years, and was, in his turn, succeeded by John Sheard in 1970 who had been his assistant since 1966. The resident agents had important and responsible positions, which meant that they would often become involved in the social life of the community in addition to their work duties.

The 1970s signalled a great period of change in the management of the Bolton Abbey Estate. The Duke of Devonshire was aware of the social need to open up the Estate to public access, and to provide all those amenities that increased visitor numbers would need. The process of opening up the Estate for public use was complicated, because it was necessary to safeguard the land and its special features from undue wear and tear, to protect farming activities, as well as provide a satisfying experience for the visitor.

Today, Bolton Abbey is a very "people friendly" place to spend time which has been achieved through a process of careful planning, constant monitoring of standards, and a continuous programme of improvements. Obviously, all of this work goes on behind the scenes and most visitors are happily unaware of the army of people who manage, conserve, maintain and improve this place of outstanding natural beauty. This work has been recognised as the Estate has won many national awards for conservation, management, tourism and education. These awards include the BT Countryside for All National Award, The Phil Drabble Award for Commitment to Youth from the Forestry Authority in 1997 for providing environmental education for tomorrow's generation with a better understanding of England's woodland heritage. As a Tourism Visitor Attraction the Estate was awarded a gold medal.

The current management objectives for the Bolton Abbey Estate are designed to ensure that it functions as an integrated unit which can accommodate the needs of agriculture and forestry, alongside those of recreation, conservation and sport. Specifically, these objectives are broken down into four individual targets which are, firstly, to endeavour to sustain the Estate's economic well-being and support its associated community; secondly, to maintain the character and quality of the landscape; thirdly, to conserve the Estate's scientific and historic interests, and to provide reasonable access for the public; and finally, to protect and enhance the nature conservation interests of the area.

However, in the early 1960s the management of the Estate was in a very different position to the one it finds itself in now. In 1966 there was only one tractor – a Field Marshall – one chain saw, and the

Field Marshall tractor at Bolton Abbey

Head Forester's only transport was an ancient motorcycle. Estate lorries were very ancient or ex army vehicles and a visit to the stores revealed an unbelievable extensive store of new tyres of every size. The Priory ruins and Bolton Hall were in need of repair; most of the tenanted farms and residential property needed modernising; there were only a few paths and no visitor information; no nature trails for visitors; access for the disabled unheard of; no village hall; an unmodernised hotel; an inadequate village car park, unsatisfactory public lavatories, no helpful signs or walkers maps, a miniature village shop and little in the way of tearooms or restaurants. In fact the provision of public lavatories was a real concern, for experience quickly proved that adequate facilities were essential – and the Estate's ancient plumbing did not meet new demands. In the village there were two ladies lavatories complete with the Estate mains water but access to them was governed by a penny operated turnstile. The turnstile was often jammed by bent pennies causing much anxiety which was often followed by high-pitched voices trying to attract the attention of Estate staff. The "qualified" Estate operator had to be summoned to strip down the machine. When everything was returned to good order, besides the utter relief of visiting ladies, the Estate could once more benefit from the collection of "P" money! So in the early 1960s the running of the Estate was still a very private affair which was conducted in the traditional way. Tourism had not yet been developed as such, and the main focus for the Land Agent was the management of the Estate's agricultural, forestry and sporting interests.

The process of rejuvenating the Estate started in the late 1960s and early 1970s. At this time the Land Agent gave priority to the organisation of a programme of renovation for all farm and residential property on the Estate. At the same time a feasibility study was conducted to see if improved access could be provided for visitors, and to ensure that farmland would be safeguarded if the land was opened up for increased recreational use. An imaginative scheme was submitted by the Land Agent to the Duke, and following his agreement, the work to transform the Bolton Abbey Estate into a vibrant place to live, work and relax began.

The development scheme started with the renovation of all the farm and residential property on the Estate. The task was enormous and the work was mainly done by the Estate's maintenance staff consisting of a team of qualified plumbers, roof slaters, joiners, bricklayers, drain diggers, stone

Estate Office
Bolton Abbey

masons and plasterers. Some of the houses still had no indoor lavatories or bathrooms, many had an unimproved spring water supply and not a modern septic tank drainage system, and none, of course, had any form of central heating. The overall cost of this exercise was considerable, but the Estate benefited to some extent from grants from the Local Council and the Ministry of Agriculture for farm work. Such was the enormity of this modernising workload that outside contractors had to be engaged on some projects.

Farming on the Estate was in urgent need of modernisation, and most farms needed new or updated buildings so that they could continue to farm profitably. The development plans that related to the Estate farms had to be submitted to the Ministry of Agriculture who were in a position to provide grants for this type of project provided they fell within certain parameters. Major agricultural improvements included the provision of new steel and asbestos buildings, conversion of stone buildings to house more stock, and the construction of new silos, drainage tanks and improved individual water supplies. Wet land often meant new tile drainage schemes were necessary and the work would be allocated to contractors, and the expense shared between the Ministry of Agriculture grant, the tenant and the landlord. The drainage work was especially important as it was designed, in addition to improving land to prevent pollution especially from farms that were either close to rivers or near a neighbour's water supply.

Milk farming was the mainstay of most farms at this time, and the Ministry of Agriculture enforced rules and regulations to enhance the standard of stock buildings, shippons, the dairy and water supply. These hygiene standards ultimately meant that most farms had to be improved to meet the Ministry's criteria.

During this modernisation period, it was one of the Land Agent's overriding concerns that all the new work, especially the buildings, harmonised with fine old ones on the Estate. Unfortunately, the budgets could not be stretched to allow building in new stone as the cost was prohibitive, but there were certain ways in which modern structures could be made to blend in with the landscape. For example, the concrete blocks used on steel framed buildings needed waterproofing and were rendered in a dark colour if they were in prominent view. Timber cladding along the sides helped ventilation and visually softened their outlines. Quantities of second hand stone were used for more prominently placed buildings when it was available. Additional tree planting could also help to disguise the outline of new buildings.

Devonshire Arms Country House Hotel, Bolton Abbey

The Estate is an ever evolving entity. Its existing activities have to be looked at and assessed in the light of future possibilities as these present themselves from time to time. For instance, when a large established farm becomes unexpectedly vacant a rare opportunity for change occurs. When this happens a full study is conducted on how the land and buildings could best be used. On one occasion when this happened one prospect considered was that the Devonshire family could take over the property and develop a Home Farm. This idea had some attractions as the Home Farm at Chatsworth was already established and successful. However, the Duke was particularly aware that farmland in the Wharfe valley was very much in demand, and he decided that it would be more useful if this farm was let to a local farm tenant.

With increased numbers of visitors, and especially children, the time came when a decision had to be made on whether a "children's farm" should be developed. This would have included an exhibition of local livestock breeds, farming practices like milking, and the chance to sell farm produce. This type of tourist experience was becoming increasingly popular with many estate owners as a means of attracting more visitors. However, the Devonshire family decided to go against the general trend, and preferred to encourage Bolton Abbey's unique natural countryside as the main visitor attraction. Their concern was always to promote the natural environment above man-made entertainments. In the light of this decision, the budget that would have been used to start a "children's farm" was used for a more innovative development, namely the improvement of the Estate's riverside footpaths for visitors and wheelchair access.

One interesting and fascinating improvement that occurred soon after the Duke's son came to live on the Estate was his desire to see certain improvements on the Estate's appearance. For instance, he chose a colour effectively a brand image, for all Estate's vehicles of dark grey with a cream door depicting the Estate logo. All writing paper was redesigned with the logo prominent and telephone numbers added of all the departments. Signage on the Estate was to be all in the same colour, cream or dark grey and all the lettering the same. The gamekeepers had to wear a livery of the same tweed suits, and particularly on shooting days, and all employees could wear an Estate tie. The Estate commissioned its own mobile radio so that contact with all the staff was always available from the Estate Office base, or between individual phones over the entire Estate.

One outstanding development was the total refurbishment and extension of the Devonshire Arms Hotel in the 1980s. The long standing tenant had retired and the Duke decided to update the hotel and form a management company to run the hotel privately. The work in the hands of a competent architect, and with much personal interest and encouragement from the then Duchess, lasted about 2 years. The hotel now has 40 bedrooms, all with deluxe en suite facilities, brand new kitchens, new entrance and car park, central heating, several business meeting rooms, dedicated dining areas each with a clear theme, a very popular

Swimming pool and part of dining saloon at the Devonshire Arms Hotel

Brasserie and a separate health spa with gym, swimming pool and tennis court. The family's management of the hotel gave it a distinctive ambience and quality of service which has been acknowledged by the many distinguished awards it has been given. The present management team continue to make improvements in the way the hotel works, and the Duke and Duchess still take a lively interest in its design and décor. Each bedroom in the Old Wing was given an individual name which links it to the Devonshire family and the Estate in some way. The décor in some rooms has been chosen to enhance a particular theme. Building on the success of the Devonshire Arms Hotel, the family have purchased and developed another hotel close by, the Devonshire Fell Hotel at Burnsall, which is just beyond the borders of the Estate, and is much more contemporary with the use of vivid colours and modern art.

A further departure from the usual ways of country management came when it was decided to use part of Strid Wood for a caravan site. The caravan site was to be built on a small section of woodland that was too poor to support the growth of trees, and a place for touring visitors was badly needed in the area. The place was ideal for this purpose as it had good access to the road, was next door to Strid Wood and was well screened from view by mature trees. The site was developed and is managed by the Caravan Club of Great Britain and is one of their top 10 sites.

During this period of intense change it was essential that the management of the Estate was co-ordinated from a central point, the Estate Office in Bolton Abbey village. The Estate Office has only been on its present site since the 1960s or thereabouts, when it took over the village Reading Room premises. Initially, the Reading Room had been built by the Estate for local residents and offered daily newspapers, a library and billiard table. Apparently it was well used until after the Second World War by which time local people had found ways to go into

Skipton or Ilkley for their local shopping and entertainment. The building was enlarged in the 1970s to accommodate the increasing number of staff who were employed to help bring the Estate up to date. Recently, the premises have been further extended so that all staff can be housed under one roof.

Running the Estate at this time involved a considerable number of people who are specialists in their own field. The Land Agent was supported by a newly qualified Land Agent and the Heads of Departments: Head Game Keeper, Head Forester, Clerk of Works, Water Bailiff, an Accountant, Tourism Manager, and Ground Maintenance Manager. Each member of this close-knit management group met the Land Agent weekly to keep abreast of the day-to-day concerns of the Estate. The whole team attended major policy meetings which were held three times each year so that forward planning and evaluation of existing policies could be accomplished.

Much of the Estate's property is let to tenants and it is usual for major improvements to be carried out when a property falls vacant. Nowadays, it is often the case that when the land and farm buildings become vacant they will be let to other adjoining farm tenants on the Estate, while the farmhouse, after substantial improvements, is let separately on an Assured Shorthold tenancy, with an initial 6 month letting period which is then renewable if both parties agree.

The Land Agent has to deal with rent reviews and collect annual rents. Every three years each farm on the Estate is assessed for a review of its rent and detailed costings and budgets have to be prepared for individual farms. But 85 farms created a considerable amount of work so the Estate was divided into three sections making only a third of the farms assessed each year. This became far more manageable, and even better when the number of farms declined to 52.

"Yorkshire in Bloom" award granted to the Maintenance Team in 2004

Approved by Craven Herald & Pioneer.

The Estate Office is the centre of all things attached to the Estate, and all problems, complaints or emergencies were directed there, usually over the telephone.

Top pictures: Barn conversion in Eastby to new cottage

As Land Agent I had to deal with all these and a lot of time in a resident agent's life is spent on trivial matters. Often such tasks could be passed to the relevant head of department – building matters, tree problems, moorland trespass, and so on, but often I would deal with it myself to establish a quick solution especially for the urgent cases. Experience of certain local tenants or other neighbours was certainly helpful, and I am extremely pleased that in the last fifteen years I have not received any calls requesting attention to a leaking roof in either house or barn!

A great deal of time had to be spent in the office dealing with technical matters, letters requesting approvals, serving notices and reporting facts etc., but time also had to be spent outdoors seeing what the various departments were doing, or when new work was required, whether it was in the woodlands, building repairs, new water supplies, pollution of water supplies, a trespass problem on the moors, and quite often daytime was never enough so the evenings were the only time to see and become aware of the current situations.

Bottom picture: The village shop constructed at Bolton Abbey in 1998

The Estate is also involved in conversion work when old buildings, such as barns and outhouses can, with planning permission, be converted into residential accommodation. In these circumstances, the Land Agent estimates the full cost, applies for planning permission and secures the budget for the conversion. Commercial property letting has also increased as an activity on the Estate and now significant income from modernised let property can be re-invested in other aspects of the business which needs financial support.

Fortunately, either from its own resources or by approved loans from its Head Office, the Estate has been financially secure enough to support local building projects that have enhanced the quality of life for those living in Bolton Abbey and the surrounding hamlets. These projects have, of course, improved the capital assets of the Estate. The new village hall, however, at Bolton Abbey is an example of a capital project funded by the local community and the local residents. Initially the Estate was approached by the thriving Women's Institute and asked to consider the possibility of building a village hall. The idea was accepted and the community set about raising the much needed finance. Remarkably the target was reached after five years running Country Fairs and a Charity shop in the village which was all staffed by Estate employees and local residents on a volunteer basis. This village hall was officially opened by the Duke of Devonshire in 1980 and it has been used enthusiastically ever since. This building, has I believe, improved life considerably as it has provided a focal point which brings people together for events from every corner of the Estate. Certain events, like the Christmas concerts and pantomimes have been so popular that an extension had to be added a few years later to provide a permanent stage with dressing rooms.

The upkeep of the Estate's buildings takes the largest slice of its annual budget as all the property has to be maintained and where necessary improved or redeveloped. Mr. Leslie Gore, the principal Clerk of Works is able not only to organise all routine property maintenance, but prepare plans for, estimate the cost and manage all extensions and new developments. His training and interest in rural buildings, some medieval, some modern, has been to the great advantage of the Estate. Even though there is a routine maintenance schedule that ensures every building receives attention in turn, emergencies do sometimes occur, which the Land Agent has to deal with as a matter of urgency. This usually happens when the weather has been inclement and on one occasion the Land Agent was called upon to rescue an elderly gentleman. His Sunday morning was interrupted by the telephone ringing and a distraught lady saying "Mr Sheard, please will you come and deal with our roof. It's raining in all over granddad's bedroom. We can't move the bed to any part of the room now to keep him dry. He can't live much longer wet through like this. Can you come and see to it?" Naturally, this call was given emergency status and the roof was repaired within a fortnight.

The Land Agent's role in this contemporary management climate is multifaceted; while the traditional role of rent collector from farms, commercial and residential property tenants and advisor to the landowner still remains, the modern working environment means that this person also has to have a thorough knowledge of a wide range of subjects. The role demands expertise in modern farming methods and conservation procedures; finance including the availability of grant aid from local, national and European sources and tourism development; public relations and marketing and the increasingly complicated laws that relate to any aspect of the Estate's many activities.

Like many other traditional jobs in the countryside that of Land Agent has increased in complexity with those employed in this area having to become more outward looking in order to ensure that the Estate survives as a viable proposition in the modern business world.

Today the Estate is responsible for 144 residential properties, 52 farms (all let to tenants) and 27 commercial premises, including the two hotels. It employs more than 150 people, and supports a community of over 1200 people. It owns 7 miles of the River Wharfe and has designated 85 miles of footpaths open to the public. It has 5 Sites of Special Scientific Interest.

What is so often forgotten is that the countryside is home to people with a range of traditional land-based skills. Farm workers, farmers, agricultural contractors, foresters, game keepers all have a major impact on the management of rural land. Their activities may seem insignificant but the results of their work is often highly visible, and it is still the case that the bulk of the Estate's income comes from its tenants. The Devonshire family have always been aware that their management of the Estate can affect people's livelihoods, and that Bolton Abbey's beautiful uplands have been shaped by hill and game farming, while the lowland woods owe much of their splendour to successful forestry management. While non-agricultural activities play a more active role, it is accepted that the Estate must continue to support the agricultural community in order to achieve balanced benefits for all.

Left:
Bolton Abbey Village Hall

Right:
Bob Middleton a stone waller always in demand

SOME HISTORIC YORKSHIRE BUILDINGS

It has been said that the land around Bolton Abbey has been occupied continuously by mankind for at least 1000 years, but there are in fact traces of human occupation from the Stone Age, the Bronze age and Roman Times. The Domesday Book makes references to settlements in Bolton Abbey, Beamsley, Drebley, Halton East, Embsay and Rylstone. Although Bolton Abbey has no grand house as its centrepiece, the variety of buildings on the Estate is one of its major attractions. Many are built in traditional Yorkshire stone with either grey slate or dark blue Burlington slate roofs, and span the centuries dating from 12th century Priory to the present day. Some of the oldest buildings are "listed" as being of special architectural interest, with four holding Grade 1 status, and sixty four buildings and structures with Grade 2 status.

The Estate is responsible for the maintenance and conservation of all the buildings within its boundaries, and especially those of historic and architectural interest. Many buildings contribute to the scenic value of the Estate as far as the visitor is concerned but the most significant ones from an historical point of view are the Priory ruins, the Boyle Room, the Rectory, the stone aqueduct which crosses the road near Bolton Hall, Bolton Hall, the Tithe Barn, Barden Tower ruins, and Barden Chapel and Priest's House.

The Priory at Bolton Abbey has a distinct appeal to visitors as it lies in its wonderful rural setting beside the River Wharfe. The site has captured the imagination of artists like J M W Turner, Girtin, Landseer, Royle and many others. Writers and poets, like Wordsworth and the Brontes found inspiration and enjoyment here too. Wordsworth inspired by the beauty of the Priory and local legend describes how a doe made a weekly pilgrimage across the moor from Rylstone to Bolton Abbey to stand beside the grave of his master. In the 16th century Richard Norton lived at Rylstone with his nine sons and daughter, Emily. Now-a-days only the watch tower remains of their fortified house, from which the Nortons took an active part in the "Rising of the North". Some of the family were executed at York for their part in standing against the king, but one son, Francis escaped, but was later caught and killed by a troop of the king's cavalry. Francis was buried at Bolton Priory. Emily, the sole survivor of the family visited the tomb frequently accompanied by a white doe which Francis had given her. After her death the doe was often to be seen around the Priory ruins and by Emily's grave. Wordsworth's poem "The White Doe of Rylstone" describes the event thus –

> "But most to Bolton's sacred pile,
> On favouring nights she longed to go,
> there ranged through cloister, court and aisle,
> attended by the soft paced doe,
> nor did she fear in the soft moonshine,
> to look upon St Mary's shrine,
> nor on the lonely turf that showed,
> where Francis slept in his last abode."

"The White Doe of Rylstone" by J.W. Inchbold (1839-1888)

Approved by Leeds City Galleries and Walter Scott

So this building seems to encapsulate what is special about the surrounding landscape which has been shaped equally by nature and man.

The Priory was begun in 1154 and its founders, the Augustinian Canons thrived there until the Dissolution of the Monasteries in 1539. At this time, Prior Moon, pleaded with Henry VIII to keep the nave intact as this part was used by the local people for worship. Henry VIII agreed, and the building became a parish church which is much loved and supported today now being part of the Bradford Diocese.

The Church has been graciously restored over several generations and much of it paid for by its patrons, the Dukes of Devonshire. 'The 6th Duke commissioned Augustus Pugin, the noted Victorian architect, whose work features in the Palace of Westminster, and who had already worked for him at Lismore in Ireland, to design new windows on the south side of the building. The design drawings for the project were exhibited at the Great Exhibition in 1851. The windows, which were painted by John Crace in 1853, are certainly thought to be one of the outstanding glories of the Church.

The 7th Duke made more substantial alterations to the building. Under his instruction, the architect, George Street, FRS, repositioned all the pews so that they faced east, moved the timber rood screen to the west end, built a new east wall without windows in 1877, installed a splendid new organ in 1880 and further windows were reglazed. This work took almost 20 years to complete, starting in 1866 and finishing in 1885.'[7]

By the 1980s the Church was in need of attention again. An impressive fund of £300,000 was raised by public subscription of which £30,000 came from the congregation, for a major renovation programme. This far reaching project was masterminded by the Rector, Canon Maurice Slaughter and, local architect, Neil Hartley; the south windows were fully renovated with new mullions installed, the roof releaded, the floor beneath the pews relaid in wood, the Victorian tiles replaced with Yorkshire flagstones, the entrance porch was roofed over and its west window glazed for the first time, the organ totally renovated and extended, the church bell restored and central heating installed. In 2004 the Priory Church celebrated its 850th anniversary as a place of Christian worship, and is still attracting a congregation of around 180 people each Sunday.

The Priory ruins have survived as a major attraction and the Estate organised their renovation in 1980s when some stonework collapsed from above one of the windows. At the time English Heritage insisted that it would only be possible to make the fault safe from further collapse, rather than replace the stone which had fallen. All the ruined walls were made safe at this time, also an information plaque installed to help visitors appreciate how the Priory would have looked when complete. The Estate continues to be responsible for the Priory ruins and grounds while the Parish Church owns and maintains its building and graveyards.

Bolton Priory in snow

©Priory Church

The Boyle Room which adjoins the Rectory (the former Boyle School) is believed to be a former Saxon chapel and was restored with funding supplied by Robert Boyle, the 7th son of the 1st Earl of Cork. He was the eminent scientist who propounded Boyle's Law in 1662. This law, remembered by many from school days, states that "the volume of a fixed mass of gas is inversely proportional to the pressure at a constant temperature"!

Robert Boyle also provided the money for the foundation of a boys grammar school which was named after him. The Boyle School is a fine 17th century building which is distinguished by its size and position overlooking the Wharfe valley. Now renamed the Rectory, it has been carefully divided into two dwellings to provide the main house for the Rector of the Priory Church, and a self contained, two bedroom flat. At the time it was built rainwater was considered to be of great value to the occupants of the house, and a device was constructed that allowed the rain to be collected from the roof. Today some of the roof water still discharges through the inside of the house but happily has been diverted to the cellar drain.

The Boyle School built in 1700 now occupied by the Rector of Bolton Priory Church with the Boyle Room at the side

The house boasts an excellent cellar which can still be used today for the storage of coal and wine. A past Rector was in the habit of making his own wine and revelled in its quality. He told many stories about canons in black gowns which he had seen walking through the cellars, and also officers in uniform horse riding through in the direction of the Priory. It would appear that his wine recipe was perhaps a little strong!

The building now known as Bolton Hall is really an "improved" gatehouse and was the original fortified entrance to the Priory, which was designed to protect the Canons from Scottish raiding parties. The 6th Duke of Devonshire instructed Joseph Paxton, architect and gardener from Chatsworth, (who was later to design the Crystal Palace) to enlarge the building, and it has since provided the dukes with accommodation for him, his family and guests.

Bolton Hall is a warren of corridors and rooms, and was a dour, dark place until in the 1970s the Duchess decided to paint the interior walls and woodwork white. An Estate workman visiting for the first time, took two handfuls of gravel from the drive with him and left a trail from the front door to his workroom on the first floor. Unfortunately, the housekeeper seeing the mess immediately swept up all the stones and the workman was totally lost in the house. His cries of "help" were eventually heard by the housekeeper, who came to his rescue and escorted him out of the building.

In recent years, instigated by the 11th Duke, Bolton Hall was fully modernised with a much improved heating system, the installation of showers and an updated kitchen. It was also reroofed as rain water was known to percolate onto the billiard table quite often at evening times. The 11th Duke always enjoyed staying here because it was a complete break and contrast from the grandeur of Chatsworth.

The Tithe Barn in Bolton Abbey village is another historically significant building on the Estate. It is understood that there were three buildings of this type on this site in the 1500s when they were used to store corn, hay and provide stables and cattle pens for livestock. Only one and a half of these Jacobean buildings remain today and the structures, amazingly, have no nails to hold the beams and joints together. All the wooden joints are held by wooden wedges and pegs. The main barn is roofed with grey slate (sandstone) covering an area of 1248 square yards and weighing approximately 124 tons, and is perhaps one of the largest barns in Yorkshire. Apart from adding roofing felt to assist weather proofing the barn remains as it was when it was built. Even the side walls take no part in carrying the weight of the barn roof as they are merely panelling and it is now used by the Estate as a modern workshop.

Tea Cottage Bolton Abbey formerly a Cruckbarn and two cottages

Bolton Hall
Bolton Abbey
painting by
Sheila Hersey
1988

Photographed by
Sycamore Studios,
Skipton

The remaining "half barn" was initially converted in 1880 into two picturesque cottages in the village. Each dwelling had 2 bedrooms, a living room, kitchen and outside toilet facilities. Unfortunately, the bedroom windows had to be constructed above the substantial roof purlins and that was at least 6 feet above the floor level, so the residents could not see anything out of these windows except the sky! When the cottages became vacant in 1977 it was decided that the building should be converted for another use. It was re-designed by joining both homes together and removing one staircase. A new dormer window was added which looked directly towards the Priory and the river, which means that there are now wonderful views from both ground and first floors.

This transformed building became the "Tea Cottage" café, which the Estate equipped with a new kitchen, suitable furniture, crockery, cutlery and appointed a manager to run the operation. At this time, the Land Agent was commissioned by the Duchess of Devonshire to find the perfect scone that could be baked for "Tea Cottage" customers. Charged with this onerous duty, he spent several weeks visiting tearooms throughout Yorkshire until he eventually decided on a particular favourite. A sample was then presented to the Duchess for her approval who agreed that this recipe produced a quality scone fit to grace the Estate's premier tearoom!

The house and the Aqueduct positioned close to the

old Gatehouse to the Priory has seen some changes over the years. It is now a farmhouse although it was formerly the local inn. Its underground cellars used to be at ground level, but at some stage the adjoining road was raised, a bridge over the stream added and an aqueduct built to carry water over the road to the adjoining mill. Nowadays no water flows over the aqueduct but it remains there, its centre arch having been raised to 10 feet 9 inches high. This still prevents large lorries and buses passing through and reduces the road width to a single track at this point.

'The Cavendish Memorial Fountain was built to commemorate Lord Frederick, second son of the 7th Duke of Devonshire having once been Gladstone's private parliamentary secretary he became the Financial Secretary to the Treasury. Ireland was becoming a major headache but Gladstone switched to conciliation, coercion was abandoned and political suspects freed. The Duke strongly disagreed, so did the chief secretary for Ireland who resigned, but Lord Frederick felt differently and accepted the post. In 1882 on 5 May he with Earl Spencer, the Lord Lieutenant of Ireland set off for Dublin bearing a "message of peace" from Mr. Gladstone.

Lord Frederick Cavendish was savagely slaughtered in Phoenix Park on the Saturday evening, only a few hours after his arrival in Dublin to undertake the duties of the Irish Secretary. Mr Burke, the Under Secretary was also fatally wounded. None of the proscribed Irish organizations admitted to it. Eventually six Irish men were later convicted but their motives were never properly explained and it seems almost certain that Lord Frederick was murdered by mistake as the murderers had not known who Lord Frederick was."[8]

'Three miles up river, Barden Tower, a stalwart and imposing ruin with a long and romantic history is situated in an exquisite position overlooking the Wharfe. Barden means "the valley of the wild boar" in Anglo Saxon and hunting was certainly very popular in those times. The Tower was originally one of seven lodges in the valley which housed men

Memorial Fountain on behalf of the late Lord Frederick

Barden Tower occupied by Henry 10th Lord Clifford in 1485 until 1523

who looked after timber and game in the forest. It was home for the Verdurer, Regarder, Agister and Woodward, as well as the Wainmote Court which heard cases relating to forest laws, as poaching legislation was strictly enforced at this time. The Verdurer looked after the valuable game and timber and so was in an important position. The Regarder made a survey of the forest every three years and recorded any encroachments on its boundaries, or trees felled without permission, and checked those people with bows and arrows and dogs. The Agister supervised the cattle which came into the forest for pasture, and pigs when fed on acorns and for which he collected fees. The Woodward was in charge of the timber.

Offenders against the forest laws were brought to the forest courts, the Woodmote and the Swainmote held at the Verdurer's Lodge at Barden Tower. Fines paid by the guilty must have been a regular income for the lords of the forest. It also provided a refuge for local inhabitants when raiding parties from Scotland looted the lands roundabout.

In 1310 the Cliffords came into possession of Barden but not until 1485 was the Tower occupied by their family when Henry, 10th Lord Clifford, the "Shepherd Lord" made it his home. Henry Clifford had spent his early life hidden in the Cumberland Fells living with shepherds as his father was a sworn enemy of the Yorkist kings, but when Henry VII became king in 1485, the Cliffords were reinstated in their lands. The "Shepherd Lord" then chose to live at Barden in preference to the grandeur of Skipton Castle. He enlarged the hunting lodge and built the chapel adjoining the Priests House. Sir Walter Scott described the "Shepherd Lord" as:

> "Most happy in the shy recess
> of Barden's lowly quietness
> and choice of studious friends had he
> of Bolton's dear fraternity".

The "Shepherd Lord" shared an interest in astronomy with his friends the Canons at Bolton Priory. In 1513 he led a band of men who fought at Flodden Field; a pike and halberd found in the Tower are believed to be those used in this battle.

Lady Anne Clifford was born at Skipton Castle in 1590, and her mother when staying at Barden, had a peculiar dream. This dream mysteriously suggested that she would loose her two sons, but her daughter would thrive and inherit all the family estates. Surprisingly, this came true in every respect, as Anne Clifford contested the normal title rights vigorously for over half a century. Then all the male heirs died, and she gained possession of the whole estate in the mid 17th century. During this period she extended Barden Tower and this is commemorated by a plaque which has been placed at the entrance to the building. Lady Anne was also responsible for finishing the almshouses at Beamsley that had been started by her mother. The central round chapel is unique, and the rooms surrounding it were built for poor widows. It is now in the care of the Landmark Trust who let it out as holiday homes. In 1676 Lady Anne died and

Beamsley Almshouse

Photograph by M. Campbell Cole Pateley Bridge

Barden then moved into the possession of the Earls of Cork and Burlington, and so via marriage to the Devonshire family.[9]

Since the late 1960s there has been a restoration and maintenance programme for the buildings on the Estate which has included extensive work being done to the ruins at Bolton Priory and Barden Tower. This has been very successful both at improving the environment for those who live there, and increasing the area's attractiveness to tourists. There is no doubt that imaginative property development has enhanced the Wharfe valley and deepened its inspiring allure.

NOTES

7 Information from "Bolton Priory and its Church" by Peter Watkins. P.88 and 90

8 Information from Stags and Serpents" by John Pearson P.157

9 Information from "Barden Tower, Wharfedale" by Mirabel Cecil P.1-8

AGRICULTURE IN A YORKSHIRE DALE

Owning several different landed estates in England obviously gives the Devonshire family much interest in farming. The 8th Duke (1833-1908) had a keen interest in his Yorkshire farm on the Bolton Abbey Estate. The Duke held several very distinguished positions in government, and his usual advice at Cabinet Meetings was always "far better not". 'On one occasion in the House of Lords when an orator finished his flowery speech with the words "this was the proudest day of my life" the Duke, is reported to have murmured to his neighbour, "The proudest day of my life was when my pig won first prize at Skipton Fair."[10]

In the 17th century a deer farm at Barden was established by Lady Anne Clifford and her cousin the first Countess of Burlington made another one at Bolton Park where 500 head were held until 1920. Primarily they provided fresh meat throughout the winter. Rabbits also provided winter meat and Coney Warren at Barden produced a good abundance from several acres. Dovecotes were also used and likewise at the Priory in those early days, but none exist now.

The Craven Heifer bred by Rev William Carr in 1830s

Photography by Sycamore Studios, Skipton

During the lifetime of the 6th Duke (1790-1858), his agent the Rev. William Carr became briefly of national fame when he bred an extremely large Short-Horned heifer, weighing 312 stones 8lbs and which was thought to be the largest and fattest four year old ever in England. He sold it to Watkinson & Co who took it on show throughout the country. Its name still lingers on as many of the local Inns adopted its name "The Craven Heifer". The cowshed where it was reared still exists at Bolton Abbey showing the enlarged doorway to accommodate this exceptional heifer.

Life as a working farmer on a livestock farm in Wharfedale involves strong physical work and an adventurous spirit for not only are these the basic essentials needed for looking after sheep and cattle, but also the qualities that ensure survival in a competitive world. The successful farmer in this area must understand the principles and practices of animal husbandry, as well as the operation of the national and international food industry.

Farming is an essential occupation in the country; if it ceased to be profitable in Wharfedale we would lose not only our own local food production but also the natural beauty of the valley. In reality, although the country may seem peaceful, it is a

Crag Nook farm Barden

place of hard work, where business concerns are governed by the dictates of a fiercely competitive commercial world.

Although, farming is the prime occupation in the country, its precariousness is not the only rural issue that faces us. Communities need support in order to ensure their survival, as rural post offices and schools are threatened with closure, affordable housing for the young becomes a rarity, and public transport links struggle to exist. Foot and mouth disease had a terrible affect on farming in this area, but in retrospect it has, I believe, revived a strong community spirit, amongst farming families in particular, as well as generally raising the public profile of country issues. A local charity, the Craven Trust, raised, by public support, £1.2 million to help family businesses badly affected by Foot and Mouth Disease, and who did not qualify for government compensation. We need to ensure that the country is a place for working and living. Agricultural shows are increasingly popular and an ideal opportunity to showcase country life. Farmers markets too, are now becoming fashionable, and introduce people to locally produced food at its best. The produce is attractive to customers because it is fresh, traceable and better quality than

Farm at Barden

food which has travelled long distances to the supermarket shelf. Farmers certainly have a central role to play in rural life and if we want a vibrant successful working community and control over our own food production then they need our support.

At Bolton Abbey farmers share concerns that affect their colleagues all over Britain, but there are certain issues that belong to this region alone. One of these local issues is the type of farm and land they manage, and the way this impacts on their ability to make a living. The Estate farm land has been described thus:-

"An area of enclosed land most of which is leased out to tenants. The land can be classified as meadow, pasture, rough grazing and moorland grazing – there being no arable land. All farms keep livestock and require buildings for in-wintering stock and machinery. The farms can be divided as follows: livestock rearing, dairy or mixed dairy and livestock rearing." Now with the recent downturn in commodity price the dairy sector has suffered with only twelve holdings remaining in dairy production.

In general the farms are small family enterprises that do not employ outside labour. Traditionally sons succeeded their fathers as tenants, however latterly with less income from agriculture, this trend is decreasing. The majority of agricultural holdings remain governed by traditional tenancy agreements with the average size of farm being 171 acres (69.20 hectares) much of which is hillside pasture. These agricultural holdings are marginal in the modern age of farming. Opportunities have arisen where holdings are surrendered. The land is split to favour other agricultural tenants and are let on modern Farm Business Tenancies, which allow far greater flexibility in terms of duration of tenancy and rent.

This system is now favoured by the Estate in the hope that extra land will support Estate tenants. All farm land is classed as grade 3 or 4 agricultural land from reasonable quality meadow land to hillside pasture on the moorland fringes.

At Bolton Abbey most farms have a "mixed" selection of livestock – dairy cows, beef cattle and sheep – but the breeds found in Wharfedale have been changing over time. In the past the stock held on the land were Dairy Shorthorn or Ayreshire cows, Hereford cattle, Dalesbred or Masham sheep, and pigs. Nowadays, the main breeds represented are Friesian cows for increased milk production; Limousins and Charolais for better beef; Swaledale, Dalesbred sheep for moorland grazing and mule sheep for lower pasture feeding.

Many farms have a vertical cross section of land extending from the riverside and rising to the moorland. This gives the farmers good meadow land near the river joining to good pastures, and then these often join to rough grazing fields before reaching up to the heather moors. The moorland areas (1000-1600 feet), grazed only by sheep, are mainly heather and bilberry providing good grazing areas with added mineral content. The hill farms bordering the moors are given a "stinted" number of sheep which may be grazed there in allocated areas. This means that the grazing on moorland is rationed between certain hill farms.

Approximately three quarters of the moorland is subject to common grazing rights, mainly for the Estate's own tenants. Moor grazing is exclusively for hill sheep and the common grazing has been registered under the Commons Registration Act 1965. Most field enclosures are constructed in drystone, the traditional form of walling in the Dales, but some of the lower farms have hedges and wooden fences, particularly along the roadsides. Most of the land is let to tenant farmers except for a small amount of land kept "in hand" by the Estate owners, mainly the Priory grounds, the car parks and areas for recreation.

Like most Yorkshire Dales farms, the mainstay of the Estate farms has been the production of milk with the addition of sheep and some hill cattle. This type of farming was complemented by research carried out by Professor Bobby Boutflour, who was the Principal of the Royal Agricultural College, Cirencester from 1931 to 1958. As a result of his personal research the management of dairy herds was substantially

Swaledale sheep

Photography by John Eveson

transformed as he discovered that by feeding cows with meal, milk yields were greatly increased. It was said of him that "he was the most capable, colourful and forceful character that ever adorned the fields of agriculture", so even as far away as Yorkshire, farmers took up his recommendations on feeding regimes for cattle. Their increased success with milk production was also helped by the Milk Marketing Board which provided collections and regular income which in turn enabled farmers to build up herds, and improve their land by additional weed control and fertilizers. When the Milk and Dairies assistance came to an end in 1997 milk farming in the Wharfe valley became very precarious. Private firms were formed to take over milk collections but the prices offered to farmers declined to such a low level that milk production for these small farms became virtually unprofitable.

Additional activities on the farm were already being tried by some tenants in 1990s and other members of the family were often able to help with business diversification into, for example, Bed and Breakfast accommodation, turkey production for Christmas markets, beef, lamb and pork production for local farmers markets, and the development of equestrian interests. In some cases on small farms, the farm tenant with no milk cows could work off the farm, at, for example, the cattle market, or a haulage firm or, started sub-contracting work for his farming neighbours, such as ploughing, haymaking, fertilizing or walling.

The farming community is the back bone, not only of the Bolton Abbey Estate, but of the whole countryside as we know it, including the National Parks. Their service to the community in shaping and tending the landscape is not done by paid employees, but by long unwaged hours of graft, in all weathers, following a craft in traditional husbandry passed on from previous generations.

It is easy to take so much for granted, yet under present living conditions there is always the threat of Foot and Mouth disease, and if it were to occur their living can be subject to total desolation. The Ministry of Agriculture try to control the disease for the farmers but also the whole countryside is placed out of bounds to visitors. The tourist trade ceases to exist and hotels, restaurants, cafes, shops, all suffer. Even the postman cannot deliver letters to the farms, and St John's Ambulance for instance that depends on voluntary donations suddenly loses a large income as agricultural shows, game shows, race meetings etc., are all cancelled.

Farmers by nature work in isolated places, and if such a tragedy does occur it is important that they are not left to fight these battles alone.

In March 2001 Foot and Mouth Disease suddenly and totally unexpectedly occurred in the countryside leaving in its wake a deserted landscape, burning pyres of animal remains and the shattered livelihoods of those who work in agriculture. It cost this country £8 billion. At Bolton Abbey seventeen farms lost valuable animals, but the majority had their stock "frozen". This meant that animal sales and the usual movement of stock around farms was prohibited, which prevented the farmers from achieving any income (except from milk production) during this period. Compensation was paid only to those who had enforced stock losses, and not to those whose businesses had been severely disrupted resulting in a large loss of income.

The legacy of this crisis rumbles on in Wharfedale and questions are still to be answered about the speed of the government's response, and why a vaccination programme was never implemented which would have saved the lives of millions of animals. So hill farming in this area, which has always been precarious, continues to be affected by the impact of the Foot and Mouth crisis as farmers struggle to build up their businesses again.

The Estate tenancy agreements which all farm tenants accept on their entry specifies how the farm land can be used. So, the agreement contains guarantees of meadowland and weed control, but does not allow tenants to open campsites or generally use their land for anything other than agricultural use. Equestrian use is usually approved as long as it remains small scale, but several small dairy farmers have now given up dairy cattle and moved towards livestock rearing and are carrying more sheep for the lamb trade. Incidentally, sheep farming which was of such commercial importance to the canons of Bolton Priory is still significant today, as 850 years later sheep dominate the fells, moorland and upper pastures. It is this activity which shapes the much loved landscape which would be overtaken by bracken and trees if the sheep disappeared from the moors.

The current price of wool is poor and in some cases it costs more to clip and transport to market in Bradford than what is earned from the selling price. However, the price of lamb meat is increasing and is a much more attractive commercial option at the moment.

Farming in this upland area often depends on the size of the farm as well as its quality of land. The Estate, has over the last 20 years, actively pursued a policy of offering land to adjoining tenants when another tenant retires. The retirement of a tenant farmer is the only opportunity that arises when more land can be offered to a neighbour, and so growth in acreage per farm occurs only in limited circumstances. In 1966, there were 85 farms, and today 52 farms exist as a result of this type of amalgamation. In 1966, most farmers made hay with only 4 or 5 on the Estate experimenting in making silage. Now all farmers make silage. This has become the usual means of producing winter food for all kinds of livestock. This change in farming practice has been caused because our summers are becoming wetter so it is proving more and more difficult to produce hay and silage making is all mechanical and less labour intensive compared to haymaking.

Most farms of over 200 acres have done well but the majority of Estate farms in this Yorkshire dale are now considered too small to provide a living for the average family. Their size was determined over 100 years ago and suitable land in the valley is a finite commodity. Today much larger farms are needed for the tenant to make a living. It is said that over 100 cows are needed to provide sufficient income for one family and on this land that means a holding of over 200 acres, rather than the usual 60 to 80 acres. So for some, farming is becoming a part-time occupation, but it is hoped that new Department of Environmental Food and Rural Affairs (DEFRA) regulations will help hill farmers to make a decent living particularly those working in the National

Woodhouse Farm painting by John Wood

Photographed by Sycamore Studios, Skipton

Park. This difficult financial situation will have far reaching consequences as the next generation of farmers will look elsewhere for careers that give them an adequate level of income. If this happens the landscape that we have come to associate with the Bolton Abbey Estate will be altered considerably, and that may have a serious impact on the ecomonic value of tourism in the valley.

Recent trends in food production are coming into question and a new approach is certainly worth full consideration in order for the "small" farmer to survive and our countryside to continue to be maintained with biodiversity and natural wildlife. Supermarkets established throughout the country have been importing food at the cost of the annihilation of our own farm produce – and I am glad to hear that recently increasing numbers of consumers are now looking for more locally produced and seasonal food.

It has been well known that "we will always need farmers" and needed now is the whole farm approach to engender the ecological care of a diverse and healthy environment with the economic demands of agriculture. Farmers are realising that they actually do need to appreciate what the general public want and it would help them if the public understood more about how food was produced to ensure sustainable consumption. In this area the annual Great Yorkshire Show provides a show case for excellent quality locally produced food.

Our British farmers do ensure food is safe, resources are carefully managed and biodiversity enhanced. None of these are guaranteed with imported food and LEAF (Linking Environment and Farming) "offers the consumer the opportunity to buy reasonably priced food which has been grown by British farmers who are committed to farming with environmental care". The LEAF marque on food allows full traceability and gives a website address to allow the consumer direct access to the farmer who produced the food.

The introduction of a programme of farmers markets in the Dales has enabled Bolton Abbey farmers to sell directly to the consumers. In fact small scale producers have a positive impact at a local level as they provide more jobs and create more wealth in the local economy. With the demand for local produce growing more farmers inevitably look at added value products for local markets and hence supplement their farm incomes. Consumer power seems to be growing and having an effect on how and what is produced on our local farms. So diversification becomes a necessity. If milk prices are falling offer bed and breakfast, or take in horses, or operate a childcare service, sell cheese or organic yoghurt or whatever is possible within the area. DEFRA tries to nurture this kind of "self help" spirit.

Farmers on the Bolton Abbey Estate are responding to this trend and contracting with local butchers to provide meat products that the public want to buy. Rare breeds of cattle, pigs and sheep are now being re-introduced to meet the demand for high quality meat.

By producing what people want, and butchering in the old time honoured way, to provide enjoyable tasty food they are turning back to what people used to enjoy in the past. This trend will most likely favour the small farmer delivering good food on a local scale. The combination of good food produced in an environmentally friendly way that in turn helps maintain the Yorkshire Dales landscape would seem to be the way forward for our rural community.

An innovative environmental farming project is being enthusiastically supported by Mr. Jim Caygill and son Jonathon, an award winning farmer at Rylstone on the Bolton Abbey Estate. The Limestone Country Project sponsored by English Nature and the Yorkshire Dales National Park, seeks to protect the outstanding beauty of the landscape in this part of the Dales, by encouraging the use of native cattle breeds to graze the limestone pastures. Jim Caygill has a herd of Luing Cattle which summer graze on the limestone pavement at Kilnsey, and winter out of doors at Rylstone. This breed was developed in the 1940s by crossing Highland cattle (28%) with British Beef Shorthorn (72%), and was registered as a breed by Cadzow brothers from the Isle of Luing, near Oban, Scotland in 1965. Luing Cattle are very hardy beasts with a placid temperament, and are excellent grazers on limestone pastures. They leave the special species of flowers and plants that grow on limestone so that the pastures return to their yester-year splendour. These cattle are slower maturing which produces excellent beef.

This successful flagship initiative is attracting a great deal of interest from other National Parks and from similar organisations abroad. The Caygills feel that using low cost native breeds, like Luing, will help in a difficult environment where beef subsidies have

Luing cattle with their owner at Norton Tower

Approved by the Craven Herald & Pioneer

been heavily cut. These shifts in farming practices are turning the clock back 40 years in grazing management i.e. mixed stocking of cattle and sheep, that he believes in the long run will give the consumer a quality product, as well as protecting the natural environment.

Some Estate farmers are also considering the advantages of establishing "organic" farms. Animals on organic farms are reared in a non intensive environment ensuring a high standard of welfare. They eat organic animal feed which is free from genetically modified products, hormones, fertilizer and pesticides. Consumers are definitely interested in this new healthy approach and the pollution caused by bracken, cleavers, and fertilizers could then be reversed, heralding a reappearance of many wildflower species and animals. Organic farming encourages farmland birds which have been lost through the destruction of their natural habitat. In the Bolton Abbey area we have lost most of the skylarks. Aided by the Royal Society for the Protection of Birds farmers could be helped to facilitate the re-introduction of farmland birds through habitat protection schemes which preserve special wildlife sites. For instance, specialist advice to individual farmers with land near moorland could help them to protect habitats of curlew, lapwing, snipe and redshank.

The Crabtree family, from Bolton Park Farm, Bolton Abbey who have farmed on the Estate for 47 years have always been interested in new methods of farm management. Steven Crabtree, the current holder of the tenancy, is committed to providing local food for local people and recently launched a new commercial venture called Bolton Abbey Foods. This initiative which has the endorsement of the Estate, aims to offer local buyers good quality meat that is fully traceable and available directly to the local consumer via butchers, restaurants, agricultural shows, farm shops, such as The Pantry at Bolton Abbey, and farmers markets.

Steven has reared a special herd of suckler cattle using the best of British native breeds combined with continental breeds. This means that the animals are ideally suited to the climate and pastures of the Yorkshire Dales. Focussing on natural methods of animal husbandry these animals are happier and healthier, and so give superb quality beef.

The same farming philosophy applies to Steven's sheep flock which graze on heather moorland and lower parklands. The breeding sheep are indigenous to the Wharfe valley, and the diverse grazing available means that they have a healthy diet, and produce a wholesome, unique meat. The farm is regularly inspected which ensures that the highest standards of animal welfare and environmental care can be monitored, and it has achieved farm assured status.

He hopes to build on the success of Bolton Abbey Foods by, perhaps beginning to rear pigs for pork, or by opening a farm shop in association with the Estate in Bolton Abbey village. Present lamb and beef sales would suggest that consumers are very willing to make the effort to source and buy naturally reared meat, even though it is not easily accessible via the usual supermarket outlet.

Today when so many people live in towns and cities there would sometimes appear to be limited understanding in the general population about country life. Farmers have had a bad press in the recent past and now have to justify their usefulness to the rest of society. Creating an environment where rural affairs can be better understood was part of the thinking behind the latest farming initiative on the Bolton Abbey Estate. Hesketh Farm Park provides an opportunity for visitors to learn about farming through hands on experience. All the animals play a vital role in this modern working farm.

The Heseltine family have been farming 600 acres of an Estate grassland farm for three generations but Chris and Sue Heseltine decided it was a case of diversifying or facing an uncertain future, and being unable to continue with traditional farming. They were making a living, but not really enough for future needs, and although saddened at not being able to totally carry on traditional farming, Sue and their children have thrown themselves into their "Farm Park", an open farm, which matured after three years of extensive research in 2005. This told them that what the public wanted most, was being able to get close to animals. The Farm Park is now run alongside traditional farming. Visitors can see

Children enjoying Hesketh House Farm, Bolton Abbey

Chris and Sue Heseltine run Hesketh House Farm

pigs, help to bottle feed the lambs and calves and get close to goats, donkeys, guinea pigs and rabbits. Tractor rides around the farm show them 1000 mule and texel sheep and suckler cows, and there is an emphasis on great experiences and having great fun. It is an opportunity to learn first hand about farming in the Yorkshire Dales.

Fortunately at the moment, the Estate farmers continue to be interested in farming as "agriculture" and are proud of their culture. This pride in tradition, landscape management, wildlife and some profit can best be seen on the small family farms that have been passed from one generation to another. This brings with it feelings

Bolton Park Farm

of pride, responsibility and continuity. The long term future of farming in the UK must continue to be based predominately on farming businesses. A sustained basis is essential to provide respectable earnings and resilience or adaptability is more achievable on this scale than in large corporate organisations. Much of the farming in the UK and Europe is largely based on family units, and there should always be a role for well run family farms. Whatever the size of farm, management depends on being realistic in business to deal with strengths and weaknesses and aim to maximise. Natural England (English Nature) even now is considering specific topics affecting farming such as funding, access, working with farmers and land managers, agri-environmental schemes, sustainable grazing and landscape, farming and rural business profitability. I definitely hope that in the future, we have farming policies that link care for the environment with the production of food, which includes a financial structure that will keep the small family farmers farming, and most of all the vision that will put the "culture" back into agriculture.

NOTES

10 Information from Stags and Serpents by John Pearson P. 165

FORESTRY

Timber has always been needed and the Canons knew this when they saw the land near the river Wharfe being offered to them as it was so important for buildings, lead mines, charcoal, bark for tanneries, and it seemed in good profusion there.

Forestry at Bolton Abbey occupies a very important place in the economy of the Estate, as timber is produced, both for its own use and as a saleable product. But the woodlands also provide a colourful landscape which forms a scenic improvement to the otherwise bare hillsides and creates essential habitats for birds, plants and animals.

Trees in Strid Wood near Barden

The woodlands lying mainly on the steep valley side slopes of the River Wharfe are an important and integral part of the landscape and can be seen from many different view points both at low and high elevations. The woodlands are of sufficient significance for the landscape quality of the Wharfe valley to warrant exemption from Capital Transfer Tax. As a condition of this exemption the Trustees of the Chatsworth Settlement prepared a Heritage Landscape Management plan for the Estate in consultation with the Countryside Agency (now incorporated in Natural England) as agents for the Capital Taxes Office. However the objectives of management need to follow a business plan which basically is:-

a) Maximise the production of sustainable timber crops.

b) Integrate the forestry with sporting, agriculture, recreation and conservation interests.

c) Conserve and enhance the character and quality of the landscape.

d) Establish the provision of a recreational and educational use in both forestry and nature conservation interests.

John Cumberland came to work on the Estate in 1984 and undertook a major restoration of all the woodlands. Woodlands need a lot of preparatory work, even five years before working on a chosen site. Details have to be submitted to the Forestry Authority branch of the Forestry Commission. Areas to be felled are walked over, photographs taken, sketches made, and felling redesigned so that their effect on visual amenity could be assessed. Wind hazards are taken into consideration on adjacent trees. Extraction routes, position of water courses, springs, pipelines to neighbouring farms, the effect of felling on shoots, pest control and deer control are all considered and the details referred to the Forestry Authority, the Yorkshire Dales National Parks and English Nature now Natural England.

When planting an area it has to be decided what will be the best species timberwise and consider also the effect it will have on the Heritage Landscape Plan.

A sample of the soil gives a good indication as to what will produce acceptable growth, and eventually there is the need to envisage what the impression of the chosen species will look like in 30 years time. An estimate of cost is established and the whole plan referred to the Land Agent for his approval. All the trees to be felled are marked, documents are drawn up for a tender and negotiations with timber merchants then proceeds. All timber is sold by competitive tender. During felling all trees felled are inspected for their marks and the stumps inspected to ensure they have been treated with urea (a precaution against a fungal attack). Before planting the felled area, all brash has to be burnt, the area rabbit/sheep fenced, and all rabbits removed from within the planting area. Roe deer control will also have to be determined to ensure they will not devastate the new young tree plants, but hopefully also survive without a culling and be redistributed elsewhere.

When purchasing new tree plants these are researched at tree nurseries regarding species, quantities, seed origins, size of plants, prices and possible discounts. Eventual orders given are for those seen as being most suitable, especially with good root systems. Since 1810 larch and Scots pine have been planted in mixtures for good volume of timber, a useful product for the Estate and for sales, and for acceptable landscape value, i.e. for nearly 200 years.

The conifer plantations were placed on poor land on the higher valley sides where there were rough boulder strewn soils, or where the farms needed shelter. However, broadleaved woods are situated on moderately fertile soils derived from boulder clays overlying millstone grit on, or near, the lower slopes of the valley. The origins of some woods in the southern part of the Estate come from long established woodlands now classified as "ancient woodland or semi-natural ancient woodland". In the northern area of the Estate the woods were created on the poor hillsides reaching 1000 feet (308 metres) in places, perhaps as landscape planting. Major planting took place between 1810 and 1820 when 3,913,629 trees were planted. The two main species grown were European Larch and Scots pine, favoured because they grew well at this altitude in a northern climate, and the timber was useful on the Estate. Many miles of substantial stone walls which have become a feature of the landscape were built so that the trees in each plantation were protected from sheep and rabbits. In general, management objectives now, to realise the commercial value of timber, have greater weight in the coniferous plantations than in the broadleaved woodlands, where amenity and conservation objectives have a greater, but not exclusive importance.

A forester usually loves to work in the country because of the hills and scenery, the fresh air, wildlife, the physical work and the fact that no two days are ever the same. The working year is governed by the seasons, so in the spring, after the long winter, foresters start weeding commercial plantations as the young trees and weeds compete for light and nutrients. Bracken is particularly aggressive and will totally smother young plants if not weeded regularly. The trees are also checked for insect and rabbit damage, particularly Large Pine Weevil (Hylobius abietis) where conifer planting follows the previous conifer crop as they feed on the thin bark, and both are serious pests on young tree growth. During the summer, weeding continues in the young plantations, and preparations for planting new stock in the areas of felled woodland start. Rabbit proof fencing must be put up to protect the trees from rabbits and sheep, and clearing drainage ditches are summer activities. The autumn brings the harvest of timber by felling in selected areas of the plantations. This time of year is also ideal for the planting of new trees and, at Bolton Abbey, on average 10,000 to 20,000 are planted most years in late autumn. During the winter planting continues weather permitting, and thinning so necessary to improve the capital value of the woodlands and clear felling is in full swing preferably when the ground is hard following a frost, as cold weather makes it easier to extract the timber. Rabbit and grey squirrel control is a concern as these animals can kill young trees if they are left unprotected.

During the second world war, about 200 acres of woodland was felled as the Estate's contribution to aeroplane manufacture because larch was badly needed for building Spitfires. Being war time this land was never re-planted and is now a conservation area dedicated to partly new woodland with the encouragement of native hill plants, also waders but particularly to the reintroduction and breeding programme for Black Grouse which is sponsored by Natural England, the Yorkshire Dales National Park and the Forestry Commission.

The Estate's woodlands which today cover approximately 1535 acres (620 ha) in 22 woodlands have been managed since 1958 under various Forestry Commission covenants and grant schemes which ensures that they will be managed and maintained as a permanent feature of the Estate, and makes the area eligible for grants which aid forestry development. The management, agreed with the Forestry Commission, is subject to a Plan of Operations which is updated every 5 years and a 20 year plan which outlines the future policy. The primary objective of the coniferous woodlands is to follow a silvicultural system of best management, (the growing and tending of trees) within a visually pleasing landscape. This system has led to the introduction of new species such as Norway Spruce, Sitka Spruce and Douglas Fir in order to increase productivity. The broadleaved, or hardwood, area of woodland have a great continuity and conservation value and are managed under a group felling or stem by stem selection with 120 or 150 year rotation. This management system is ideally suited to the multiple objectives of conservation, landscape, amenity, and timber production.

Sycamore and Ash are the main timber producing hardwood species grown on a rotation of 70 to 80 years. The variety of species grown within the broadleaf woodland means that a diverse woodland habitat can be maintained under a continuous cover system.

In all these woodlands early and adequate thinning of plantations takes place to encourage growth and the thinnings produce the first return of timber sales, usually as fencing posts. To encourage sales the Estate established a pressure treatment plant for conifer thinnings which increased the sales as well as the price for this "preserved" timber post and ran successfully for 7 or 8 years. To protect the trees from damage, the tenant farmers and foresters keep the area free of sheep and rabbits using stone walls and fencing. They also need to control grey squirrels and keep an eye on the ever expanding population of roe deer. The beautiful red squirrel which would be a welcome inhabitant of the woodlands is no longer found on the Estate. This species is sadly missed, especially as the dominant grey squirrel does so much damage to trees and wildlife.

The grey squirrel is dominant throughout Britain

The Red Squirrel. Inset: The Grey Squirrel

Approved by the European Squirrel Initiative

because it was introduced from America between 1870 and 1926. It has become a major pest as they strip bark off sycamore and young trees, distorting their growth and normal shape, take eggs and young from woodland birds, such as finches, tawny owls, nuthatch and compete with them for limited food supplies. They also eat the eggs of game birds and take their chicks too.

Grey squirrels impact on the indigenous red squirrel population which has almost totally disappeared. Apparently, it is estimated that there are only 30,000 red squirrels still surviving in Britain but almost 2 million grey squirrels populate these isles. Britain is now setting up twenty heavily protected red squirrel sanctuaries and recommending strict controls on the grey squirrel population. I hope

Timber extraction Strid Wood, Bolton Abbey about 1929

Painting by Rosemary Lodge photographed by Sycamore Studios, Skipton

that this will save the red squirrels from extinction in the north of England as they do little harm to trees or wildlife, and hopefully the Estate will be able to make a considerable contribution to this conservation initiative.

The Estate foresters survey the woodlands regularly to check for disease, such as Honey fungus, insect, vermin, roe deer damage and natural ageing or wind damage. Currently, a disease affecting Horse Chestnut trees is spreading throughout the north of England and it has arrived at Bolton Abbey damaging some of the tree stock, but the Forestry Commission thinks the damaged trees will survive.

Strid Wood is ancient and has always been the most enjoyed of the Estate's woodlands because it represents what a wood is meant to be – a collection of fine growing oaks, beech, sycamore and ash, combined with the outstanding beauty of its natural plant life, bird and insect populations. There are wood anemones, violets, wood sorrel, early purple orchids, bluebells, and some rare plants, lichen and fungi which are of great botanical interest. The wood is particularly important for lichen species and it is the best lichen wood in Yorkshire, several being very local in distribution and nationally rare.

The wood is highly valued by naturalists who carry out regular surveys every year, in particular on the populations of plant and insect species. Previous Head Foresters have also been keen to plant some unusual tree species which grow well in this wood. Woodland management programmes have had to take account of the important natural history of Strid Wood, and in 1985 the Nature Conservancy Council (now Natural England) demonstrated their interest in this area by designating it a Site of Special Scientific Interest (SSSI) and it also happens to hold the largest example of acidic oak woodland within the Yorkshire Dales.

The Estate produced a detailed management plan which is reviewed every five years. This has included stem by stem enumeration of all trees which produces valuable information on species, type and intensity of thinnings to be made and the degree of natural regeneration occurring.

Today the aim is to safeguard the important flora within the woodland and to gradually transform the wood back to a native oak and ash woodland naturally although this may take at least two centuries to achieve.

However, the Estate was also keen, while preserving the flora and fauna of this wood, to allow public access to it for recreational purposes, as the main paths, carriage way, seats and view points were originally opened to the public by the 6th Duke of Devonshire in 1810 or thereabouts and have been used by visitors ever since. Interpretation of the many and varied aspects of this woodland and its management is considered very important by the Estate. New nature trails, high and low level paths

A felling, strimming, cutting machine of 460hp very useful for thinnings

with seats were created and views were re-established in 1986 as part of a thinning programme. The Estate was able to increase the number of native species of trees represented in the wood by planting in the gaps opened up by thinning. An additional woodland has been established when a new 9 hectare area was planted with native species of trees and shrubs at Barden including oak transplants produced from acorns of 70 of the best oak trees in Strid Wood. This also provided a quiet area away from the public where roe deer could settle and graze without interference.

Sessile oaks within the wood have adapted to the site over thousands of years and the Estate collects acorns during mast years. These are then sent to a forest nursery to be grown on into two year old transplants, which are then planted in Strid Wood or other areas on the Estate. This will safeguard this important origin of Sessile oak for the future.

The high standard of the Estate's forestry was recognised 1996 when Strid Wood won the Forestry Authority's Centre of Excellence Award for the best woodland in the north of England. This encompassed; improving the quality of the landscape, creating benefits for wildlife, providing access for people and growing timber in environmentally sound ways. Strid Wood was judged to be an outstanding winner and beat 11 other competitors for the title. The judges commented that this woodland had a "huge sense of place, no litter and an innovative programme of improvements carried out within the Estate budget". They noted that "there was a good volunteer programme, a degree of privacy and conservation, which allows 84 breeding bird species to nest, including dippers and spotted flycatchers".

This ancient woodland was established by natural regeneration thousands of years ago. Over the centuries the character has changed due to the introduction of trees such as Beech, Douglas Fir, and Larch for the production of timber but is firmly established as a Site of Special Scientific Interest woodland beside the River Wharfe. It receives over 100,000 visitors every year, has two car parks, an information point, a school room and six miles of maintained planned paths with facilities for the disabled. Stone built pits, dated from the 1800s, were found adjacent to the boundary wall and are believed to be the earliest rabbit traps ever found.

In 1984 the Estate appointed John Cumberland as the Head Forester, who had worked with Ronnie Rose an expert in wildlife management. Between them they encouraged wildlife to flourish on the Estate by the planting of broadleaved trees which are particularly attractive to song birds. Their maxim that countryside management should always work with nature not against it benefited both the forestry and wildlife on the Estate, and won them many accolades. Their innovative practices were widely copied both in this country and abroad. Using John's experience a Forest Trail, called the Cumberland Trail after its founder, was developed in Strid Wood with interpretation boards explaining flora, fauna, tree identification and how the forest is managed. The information barn includes a TV size screen showing a breeding bird on its nest nearby so that visitors can see the eggs as they hatch. The Estate still retains a member of staff who carries the medieval job title "warriner" who maintains a stable population of Roe deer and control of the rabbits, grey squirrels, and disease causing insects so that plants and wildlife occur in abundance in the woodland.

In addition to the formal woodlands the Estate is blessed with a considerable number of hedgerow trees. Sycamore and ash have been planted in groups to shelter farmhouses and farm buildings, and specimen trees can be found at Beamsley, Hawpike Farm, the Bolton Abbey avenue and near the Priory. The Priory trees were all donated by members of the public as memorial trees and are all maintained by Estate foresters. All the trees throughout the Estate belong to the landowner, so maintenance and their removal and replacement is a task borne by the forestry staff. It is particularly important to survey trees in public access areas regularly, including for instance, public footpaths and roadsides, to ensure public safety.

Within recent years the main species planted in plantations has been Sitka Spruce on high land, Douglas Fir in selected areas, European Larch and

Hybrid Larch (a cross between European and Japanese Larch). All are capable of high volume growth and provide excellent building timber and pulpwood respectively to meet the nation's need for more timber.

The improved commercial demand for Christmas trees during the 1980s encouraged the Estate to diversify into this activity by establishing a plantation for growing Norway Spruce trees. An ideal location was found at the northern entrance to Strid Wood so that customers would have car parking facilities and access to a small shop. Every year at the beginning of December the sale area opens complete with a marquee seasonally decorated, for the sale of holly etc., where mince pies are served to customers as they wait for their tree to be made ready for them. The success of this enterprise lies in the fact that people can walk into the plantation to select their own tree, have it cut down or dug up for them, and then wrapped in a netting to facilitate transporting it home in or on their car, and so a trip to Bolton Abbey becomes part of their Christmas routine. The idea was extremely successful until the early 2000s when non-needle drop trees such as Nordman Fir became popular, as they held their needles better in centrally heated homes.

Trees have grown in this part of the Wharfe valley since the Ice Age – and the oldest tree on the Estate is believed to be the Laund Oak which grows on the roadside halfway between Storiths and Barden. It is estimated to be about 750 years old. Some believe that an oak tree can live for 400 years, and then takes 400 years to die! The oak trees at Bolton Abbey are predominantly Quercus petraea – Sessile oak, not the more common English oak, Quercus pedunculata. This specie is particularly suited to the Estate because it is hardier and tolerates less rich soil as well as being more resistant to mildew and Tortrix caterpillars.

Christmas trees adjacent to Strid Wood, Barden

The Estate is keen to promote the benefits of forestry as an industry to those who live in the area and particularly to children, many of whom spend most of their lives in towns and cities, and so are loosing touch with nature. Increasingly, youngsters cannot identify the leaves of traditional British trees like the oak and ash. A recent survey by the Woodland Trust showed that 94% of children were unable to identify beech and only 6% could identify ash, 20% oak and 54% holly. Of the 7 to 14 year old children questioned in the survey, 76% admitted that they spent free time

Left:
The Laund Oak believed to be 750 years old

Right:
Waterfall in the Valley of Desolation

outside shops or on waste ground, and only 14% spent time with friends in the countryside or in woods. Just over 40% had never visited a wood. Amazingly, 1 in 7 children never play in the country. So every year school children from all the surrounding schools are invited to Bolton Abbey for a free 3 day course. The programme includes activities, talks and guided tours. Each tour shows a different aspect of the Estate, and how it is managed on a day to day basis. Around 1000 children join in this exercise, and hopefully, this experience will help them to understand what happens in the countryside and perhaps consider a career related to country activities.

Since 1990, 351 acres of additional areas of woodland, outside the original Dedicated Woodland Area have now been planted, even more land with both hardwoods and conifers than any other estate in the Yorkshire Dales National Park.

Another area of the Estate has been developed recently by Roy Lingard, the current Head Forester, as a major educational opportunity to show visitors that trees have always been important and significant in this country supporting and creating a quality landscape and wildlife population.

The "Valley of Desolation", was so named when a storm in 1836 caused immense damage and uprooted most of the mature oak trees leaving a wilderness of bare ground and rough grazing for the farmers in this, a normally sheltered valley. One or two veteran oaks remain but the valley has now been restored and replanted with various tree species depicting what has been grown in the British Isles since the ICE AGE.

Included in the valley is a geological trail, everything clearly visible and especially the waterfall in Posforth

Gill. Also added is a spring-fed pond, now with rushes, but of increased benefit to the bird life.

15,000 years ago tundra vegetation would be re-established and in a cooler climate willow shrub, dwarf birch and bilberry would become dominant. Wild animals would follow such as the woolly mammoth, ptarmigan, woolly rhino and wolverine. However about 8000 BC tree growth probably started: mostly birch, Scots pine, hazel, elder, elm and a few oaks. Later when the climate became warmer, broadleafed trees would fill the valley bottom mainly oak, elm and lime.

The appearance of the landscape then would be of an established woodland and populated by boar, otter, lynx, brown bear and Stone Age people.

This project has been well researched by Roy Lingard and supported by Trevor Nash, a local retired school master, who have written an educational booklet for students, and the whole scheme has been well supported by the Forestry Commission, English Nature, Yorventure, and the Yorkshire Dales Millennium Trust.

Weather permitting this "exhibition" of an ancient woodland should grow and generate great interest as the years progress. But do not forget in forestry terms maturity can take 70, 120 or 200 years!

New visitor centre in Strid Wood 2005

General view of a plantation at Barden

In 1988 the Government introduced changes in forestry taxation and confidence in the forest industry fell. Schedule D tax relief was abolished, no increases in grant aid under the Dedication Scheme coupled with increases in net costs meant that a decision to seek release from the Dedication Scheme and an application to join the Woodland Grant Scheme as at 1st April 1993 was possible.

Best forestry practices provide jobs and new income. Timber production and adding value to that timber within rural communities is of vital importance but energy from wood fuel, protection of the environment and increasing use of woodlands for recreation are already giving us new ways of providing rural areas with valuable new income.

Forestry could play a much bigger part in Wharfedale's economy as it is a complementary activity to hill farming, recreation and tourism, and ties in well with strategies for nature conservation and the maintenance of Sites of Special Scientific Interest. It can easily be woven into the fabric of the countryside to enhance the environment for those who live and work there, or those who come to visit for pleasure. This could be of particular benefit in an area of marginal land, like the wide expanses of Wharfedale, and I believe that this balance has perhaps already been achieved at Bolton Abbey. Britain as a whole only has about 10% of its land dedicated to forestry, in comparison to Germany which has 30% under tree cultivation. Should the United Kingdom work towards 30% forestry coverage it would mean that we would not be so dependant on the importation of foreign timber, and estates like Bolton Abbey, would experience a resurgence in timber production as this would start to have a real commercial value again.

Trees planted in the last ten years amounts to approximately 70,000 which includes hardwoods, conifers, amenity trees, and parkland trees.

Forestry management today involves the use of computers recording all the information on forestry work, and producing plans and forecasts as well as estimates of management costs. But reality always depends on the practical answers, as seen on the ground, and hillsides, and always subject to our British weather!

The existing woodlands comprise the following species:

Beech	0.79	Hectares
Birch	9.21	"
Corsican Pine	1.29	"
Douglas Fir	12.08	"
European Larch	120.13	"
Hybrid Larch	4.03	"
Japanese Larch	29.53	"
Lodgepole Pine	2.25	"
Mixed Broadleaf	242.00	"
Mixed Conifer	42.00	"
Norway Spruce	44.64	"
Poplar	0.53	"
Western Red Cedar	0.19	"
Scotts Pine	16.69	"
Sitka Spruce	77.85	"
Sycamore	16.22	"
Other broadleaf	0.29	"
Total	620.00	Hectares (1,535 acres)

RED GROUSE, BROWN TROUT

Although on first impressions heather moors look totally wild, really they are not. They have been subject to improvements by human activity over thousands of years. It is increasingly recognised that the future of our heather moors along with their attractive wildlife and important archaeological sites depends on their traditional use and management.

In winter the purple moor of summer becomes a hard and inhospitable place and few animals other than hardy sheep and red grouse can be found. However, in spring great changes occur, grouse are joined by large numbers of other ground nesting birds, particularly curlew, golden plover, lapwing, redshank, snipe and merlin. In August the heather comes into full bloom bringing an amazing burst of colour to the upland areas and the grouse shooting season begins. This provides an essential source of income for the Bolton Abbey Estate, and for the economy of upland communities a revenue vital to long term management of the moorland areas.

Grouse feed almost exclusively on heather and are thus restricted to the heather dominant moorlands of the British Isles. They can exist in remarkably high densities and this has encouraged landowners to manage and harvest this wild population. Measures to preserve and improve the habitat of red grouse are important, as this species has suffered a dramatic national decline because it is especially vulnerable to natural predators. A healthy population of grouse on the moors is dependant on

Red Grouse

several factors such as very little snow during the winter, low level of predators, no heavy summer storms, heather burning, a plentiful supply of streams and waterways, plenty of insects at hatching time, good grouse health giving a normal clutch size, a moderate level of shooting the previous year, good natural habitat and an acceptable density of the existing grouse.

Apart from those with a major water catchment area or a special attraction for visitors sheep farming and grouse management are the principal activities associated with heather moorland areas. Correctly managed they operate to the advantage of each other. Heather is kept young and vigorous by controlled burning always done between October and March, and on an average 10 year rotation.

Heather burning on Barden Moor

Heather roots are left undamaged by the burning and the plants are "shocked" into germinating quickly. This process provides a moor with mosaics of different aged heather all over – the oldest providing shelter and cover for grouse and other birds, the middle aged heather gives good nesting sites, and the new shoots succulent food for birds and sheep. Winter burning stimulates an abundance of fresh shoots which in turn becomes food for birds and sheep. The resultant mosaic of heather at different ages, often interspersed with streams and boggy places, supports a wider variety of wildlife than would heather of an even age.

The best moors are those that have been managed for both grouse and sheep farming over the years. Left to their own devices moors would soon be overrun by bracken (the Estate controls 250 acres per annum), invasive pine or birch scrub, significant increases in foxes, stoats, could be overgrazed by sheep and habitats for many animals and plants would be lost. Here the Estate's policy is to control bracken, prevent overgrazing and eliminate afforestation and reclaim where appropriate. Stewardship of the moors has ensured the survival of the heather. Control of predators not only protects the grouse but also the merlins and upland waders, and the Estate has been found to have a high population of waders.

The late Duke was fully aware of the diverse interests that exist on the moors and would always try to provide adequate facilities for people to enjoy and have access for these when necessary. In fact in 1968 the 11th Duke decided that the general public should have access to the moors and entered into a formal Access Agreement with the West Riding County Council, the terms of which are managed by the Yorkshire Dales National Park, and this is more fully explained in the chapter "Stepping Out of Doors".

There was one occasion when men carrying out their own detailed survey on the merlins, which entailed wandering about the moors searching for the birds, grossly interfered with the keepers control of grouse nesting. Even disparaging articles appeared in the local daily paper denouncing the work of the landowner and his gamekeeper. When the articles were seen by the Duke he decided to attend the next County Council meeting. Whatever he said remains unknown but it diffused the situation immediately; sense prevailed, the survey went ahead and was organised so that the nesting grouse were not disturbed.

To maintain and increase bird populations, keepers manage the habitat. Some drainage, and heather burning develops and increases the heather – but the previous practice of draining wet areas has been stopped now because water is essential for providing insects which are vital food for young chicks occurring most prolifically near streams and ponds. All ground nesting birds their eggs and chicks are vulnerable to predators such as the carrion crow, fox and stoat. Within the current laws gamekeepers need to control these predators so that more birds will survive. Controlled sheep farming prevents overgrazing and the ultimate appearance of coarse unwanted grasses on the moor. The traditional management of moorland in this way for grouse and sheep is the most certain way of securing its future and long term economic viability.

More than any other British game bird, the Red Grouse is a natural product of this environment. It is not hatched or reared in captivity. It is truly wild and populations survive where the habitat is suitable, predators are controlled, disease is at a low level, shooting is managed and, when necessary restricted to allow for future breeding. Measures to preserve them also benefit other moorland birds and wildlife.

Various studies on the health of grouse have been carried out and Trichostrongylus tenuis has been identified as the parasitic worm causing catastrophic death rates throughout large numbers of grouse. Sadly, the Red Grouse is its only host, and they are most prevalent in the wetter moorland areas like the Pennines. To control this parasite the Estate purchases edible sized grit fully soaked in levamisole hydrochloride, which is an anthelmintic. This is placed in heaps around the moor – and the grouse will readily feed on this. If a grouse moor is devastated by this parasite it can take several years before their numbers are restored to a healthy level.

The gamekeepers are the staff who personally devote their lives to the well-being of all the grouse, but also all the welcome ornithological wild life which come and breed on these special heather moors.

Predation control helps survival of so many species

Heather Moor at Barden

Left: Labradors waiting for instructions
Right: Lunch Hut on Barden Moor

Black Grouse painting by Archibald Thorburn

besides grouse, and the management of the grouse moors today have ensured their survival.

A day's work may involve repairing butts, cutting heather or bracken around them, maintaining walls and roads, also lunch huts, cleaning out roadside ditches, checking traps, and controlling foxes.

The Estate usually employs six gamekeepers. A Headkeeper, plus four other keepers all of whom have their own territory of moorland, approximately 3700 acres each, and pheasant or student keeper. The keepers walk the entire moorland area each year in July and count the grouse seen. This indicates to the Land Agent the approximate stock of grouse that year and then it is decided how many days shooting should follow.

The Estate has seen grouse shooting over its moors since the 1750s. The game books record the numbers shot by many illustrious guests, including Edward VII and George V who shot until 1926. Now the Duke often takes the first days available for his party of friends and relations, and then offers days that can be let by the Estate to other interested parties. A day's grouse shooting on many of the well managed grouse moors will produce a daily bag of 100 brace or more, but at Bolton Abbey 300 brace a day is often produced in August and 500 brace has been known.

Grouse shooting from the "glorious 12th" onwards is always a sociable and enjoyable occasion as so many people on the Estate are involved. Innumerable vehicles, mostly land rovers, transport the party of "guns", beaters, loaders, gamekeepers, dogs and bird cart up onto the remote parts of the moors. Each shoot consists of 5 or 6 drives – birds driven forward to the butts by beaters led by the keepers. The Estate has several different drives on its two moors so that guests shooting are unlikely to shoot the same drive twice even after three days in a shooting party. Lunches are brought to the moor and are served in special, stone and thatched "lunch huts" built for the purpose. Each shooting lunch menu is prepared according to the wishes of the shooting party. At the end of the day all the shot birds have been collected and taken to the game larder in Bolton Abbey village, which is a special building where they are counted, healthily stored on racks until sold either to a local outlet or to an agency covering the London market. As a farewell gift it is customary for the Duke to give each "gun" two brace of grouse for each day they have been shooting.

There are some years when grouse shooting is not possible due to disease which results in a lack of birds. In addition the Estate runs a pheasant shoot over half the Estate, and lets most of the remaining land to syndicates. Care is necessary and duly taken when shooting because of the abundance of footpaths, and shooting never takes place on a Sunday when the Estate receives most of its visitors.

The 11th Duke of Devonshire had wanted for many years to see Black Grouse on the moors just as he did when he was young. This species has been missing for several years, and so a special effort is being made to see if they can be re-established. A 200 acre piece of moorland was considered suitable for re-introducing this bird onto the Estate. The ground had to be prepared so that it would be attractive to breeding pairs of Black Grouse and this has been supported wholeheartedly by outside conservation organisations.

Black Grouse visit "lekking" sites between February and May where the black cocks leap into the air with bubbling cries in a battle of supremacy in their courtship. At this time they are easy to see and

count, and luckily they are already found in neighbouring Wensleydale and Swaledale. Hopefully, the Estate will succeed in attracting them back into Wharfedale, and reverse the decline in their number which started in the 1970s.

Black Grouse need a mosaic of habitats over a wide area for feeding, lekking (displaying), nesting, chick

Heather moors at Barden

Photographed by Colin Raw

Top: Grouse in flight

Photographed by Nicholas Ingram

Botttom left: Short-Eared Owl
Bottom right: Curlew

rearing, cover and shelter so foresters, farmers, moorland managers, and keepers all need to be involved to play a role in safeguarding the habitats.

The hill farms which adjoin heather moorland play a vital role in providing suitable habitats. The cock Black Grouse often chooses a lekking site on permanent pasture near the moor edge. Herb rich meadows provide a good source of year round food. Weeds provide seeds in the autumn and winter and particularly young conifer plantations (prethicket stage) suit Black Grouse for insects and nesting sites.

Mature plantations provide shelter and food, particularly well spaced native broadleaved groups but in these habitats vermin also must be controlled. They welcome semi-improved grassland on open hills, and long heather (over 40cm) for shelter, hiding females, and for feeding. Some nest on areas of rough grass, rush, sedge mosaic found on the "White Hill", along the moorland edge, and then move to the heather dominated ground in the winter.

However boggy marshy ground is vital for feeding opportunities and where possible cotton grass is an important food for hens in the spring. The wetlands are rich in invertebrates so much favoured as chick rearing habitats in summer, and rush and sedge seeds are eaten in late summer and autumn. Hence much work needs to be done to provide the ideal habitats.

Management of all the wildlife, and the many activities on the moorlands is totally achieved by the game keepers through their personal interests and devotion to duty, in an environment they know, understand, and feel at home in.

To see grouse and all other wildlife multiply year by year is a great encouragement to them, and now members of the public can walk across these moors to enjoy them too. Preservation of their particular allotted moor and all that it produces is one of the keeper's main tasks, but now the public have access, this can mean extra work and vigilance, as in a moment of thoughtlessness, say a carelessly discarded cigarette, an abandoned bottle, or the disposal of a barbecue, can cause a truly devastating fire. This can destroy remarkably quickly, all that they have achieved over many years and full restoration will take several more years to re-establish what nature intended as happened on Ilkley Moor in 2006 which lasted for 3 days before it could be controlled.

The success and achievement of all wildlife on the moorlands and their habitats is done by the committed work of the game keepers.

Shooting provides jobs and supports businesses in these rural areas. The Country Landowners Association has commissioned an independent study and this confirmed that shooting supports 70,000 fulltime jobs in the UK from game keepers to jobs in hotels, and that those who shoot spend over £2 billion each year on goods and services.

Much of this expenditure is spent in the less populated and rural parts of the country where wages are lower and there are fewer opportunities for the rural economy to diversify. Shooting does of course have significant environmental, as well as economic benefits. Two thirds of rural land in the UK is influenced by shooting and £250 million a year is spent on wildlife and habitats. This Estate does therefore share in the country's 2 million hectares of the area under conservation and habitat creation and management by shoots.

RIVER WHARFE AND BROWN TROUT

The Estate is extremely lucky to have an excellent river flowing through it with water collected from limestone country in the Upper Dale which makes it perfect for Brown Trout, Grayling and occasionally, Salmon. The Canons would certainly have taken advantage of the river salmon and historians recall ancient times when salmon ran up the river, but due to pollution down stream and several weirs no salmon are returning at the present time. The Estate manages five miles of the river in hand, and offers day and season tickets to anglers, whilst the remainder is let to the local Appletreewick, Barden and Burnsall Angling Club.

The surrounding scenery provides a spectacular backdrop for any angler and this well known stretch of water provides good fishing for novice and experienced hands alike. Fishing competitions on this river are particularly popular, and this water has been used for testing anglers for the Yorkshire team.

Fishing on the River Wharfe

Fly fishing is very popular in this part of the Yorkshire Dales so the Estate has endeavoured to create as near as possible a "wild fishery". Stocking of reared trout has been reduced to the very minimum and angling is limited to barbless hooks only and a maximum daily take of 4 trout, not less than 10 inches in size. All other fish caught are to be returned carefully to the river and these if not damaged continue to grow on. The anglers are extremely happy with the arrangements and the river contains more wild and larger fish.

In the 1960s the Estate hatchery existed in a small stone building in Storiths. Water came from a hillside spring and the bailiff, Mr Newbould, took great care to hatch the eggs and then place the fry in the River Wharfe's tributary streams. He was also known for his much demanded home made flies. However, as the popularity of fishing the river mushroomed, a larger and more efficient hatchery was needed, which could also be linked to a fish farm. So, the Estate built its own hatchery and fish farm in the 1970s using a redundant medieval site, probably last used by the "Shepherd Lord", where it is believed fish were farmed and duck were caught by being driven up a netted tunnel along one side of the pond. The upper streams of the tributaries of the River Wharfe are fed with Brown Trout fry, and fish are grown on to stock size, with surplus fish sold to local Angling Clubs. This business has now been taken over by a tenant who stocks the River Wharfe for the Estate, and has developed fish rearing as a proper business supplying angling clubs.

Improvements to the quality of fishing have always been uppermost in the mind of the Land Agent, and the decision to go for wild fish has perhaps been the most popular. The river used to be stocked generously with larger trout of takeable size, but technically the fish became lazy, were easy to catch and the sport became less interesting for the mature angler. The process of producing wild fish has succeeded and anglers are delighted with the additional challenge and when caught after much patience and the application of river science the end result is a far better fish.

The Estate managed length of the river has a footpath along both sides for the entire 5 mile stretch. Access given to walkers means that fishermen have to take care when casting. Farm cattle and sheep also graze to the waters edge but recently, the Estate took the decision to erect fences along the riverside preventing livestock from grazing the river bank and providing safer walks for people along the footpath. This measure encourages grass, weeds and shrub growth, and from the angling point of view provides a better river habitat, fly life and shade. Also it prevents erosion and makes it more difficult for the fish to see on shore activities, so the angler has a better chance of a decent catch.

The river is in good condition now but in past years the Land Agent has had to deal with bad pollution into the river caused by the Yorkshire Water Authority. Firstly the authority excavated a length of the River Wharfe bed up stream of Buckden to control river gravel, and secondly built a large extension onto the Grimwith Reservoir. Both events affected the Estate fishery and the effluent from the reservoir flowed into the River Wharfe destroying normal angling. Lengthy consultations took place and after several years of work and remedial care the cause of the pollution was corrected. The river was returned to a good condition or "gin clear" as the locals call it, which means the stoney bottom was clearly visible and the water became alive with natural flies, insects and the welcome dippers. The Estate fishery was restored and some compensation received.

Any pollution of the river or interference with fishing rights is a constant cause of concern for the Estate, and the River Keeper is the person primarily responsible for ensuring that problems are detected and corrected swiftly. The Estate Keeper who manages the whole 5 mile length of river, checks water quality, examines inflowing streams, deals with riverside vermin, keeps a look out for poachers, stocks the river and welcomes anglers.

The standard of angling is important as the river is providing such a first class facility, and the Estate wishes to safeguard this countryside activity for the benefit of all who wish to fish. But the Wharfe is not managed only for the benefit of anglers so restricted controls have to be made to allow for other uses of the river such as paddling, dinghies and swimming. A happy medium has to be achieved and this is done by sectioning off the river so that each activity has its specific stretch of water. However, angling remains the most cherished and important activity on the River Wharfe.

The river does not provide the only fishing opportunity on the Estate; reservoir water is also used for the sport. The Barden reservoirs were built by Bradford Water Corporation in the 1870s to provide water for Bradford residents and textile manufacturers, but the sporting rights, including

River Wharfe at Bolton Abbey

Barden Bridge on the River Wharfe

fishing were reserved. The water in the Upper Barden Reservoir is too acid to support fish but the Estate welcomes fishing on the Lower Barden Reservoir, and this water has been open to anglers since the 1970s. The Lower Barden Reservoir is fed by underground springs, miraculously coming from alkaline limestone, so the water is good quality and trout do very well in this environment. The reservoir is let to and stocked annually with rainbow trout by the Appletreewick, Barden and Burnsall Angling Club. The club members really enjoy this kind of fishing which is a contrast to that offered on the river.

The Estate has been extremely fortunate that the 11th Duke had a keen personal interest in the upkeep of red grouse and trout. Not only did he keep alive the family involvement with game management, his encouragement resulted in Yorkshire providing some of the best field sport in Britain. His concern for wild life and natural game has been of immense benefit to their survival in this part of the country. His willingness to share his enthusiasm with us all is a legacy that is being carried on by the 12th Duke as part of the family's commitment to safeguarding these traditional aspects of country life.

Heron, one of the many species of wildlife to be found on the Estate

Nature Conservation and Wildlife

Conservation of the landscape features such as the river and its valley, the hillsides, the extensive woodland and expanse of heather moorland, has been an important part of the Bolton Abbey Estate's multiple purpose management plan for several generations. Habitat conservation is equally significant, and has played a major role in the management of the moorlands to improve not only red grouse habitats, but also the habitat for other forms of wildlife, particularly wading birds. The conservation of Strid Wood is secured through its Site of Special Scientific Interest status and it has a special management plan agreed with English Nature to increase its natural species diversity. Sessile oak and ash in particular will be planted and allowed to regenerate over the next century or so, increasing the numbers of these species.

The Bolton Abbey area is home to an abundance of wildlife which is one of its attractions for visitors who come to see the diversity of birds, flowers, plants and insects to be found here. The variety of land, its topography, soil structure and woodlands all support many species of flora and fauna found there, and in 1993 English Nature felt that the Estate's environmental importance should be fully recorded and recognised. The Estate had virtually no records of plant life in Strid Wood, but certain

Bluebells in Strid Wood

By kind permission of Heritage Cards & Souvenirs Ltd., Burnley

individuals have made their own records, particularly Thomas Knowles (1691-1781), who worked for the Dukes of Devonshire and searched for plants at Londesbrough and Bolton Abbey. His records are with the British Museum's Natural History Publication, "No Ordinary Gardener"!

English Nature has produced amazingly detailed schedules that list all the wildlife to be found in the Bolton Abbey Estate and plans identifying areas of special interest. A great deal depends on the natural vegetation found there and in 1986 they produced a map 1/10,000 scale covering the flora and fauna interests over the unenclosed uplands and the larger hillside plantations. In the upland moor areas the ground is covered by Dry Dwarf Shrub Heath, Wet Bog, Acid Flushes, Bracken, Dry Heath/Acidic Grassland mosaic, Acid Cliffe and Rocks. On the lower hills, acidic unimproved grassland, semi-improved acidic pasture, pasture and hay meadows, all exist interspersed with woodland.

There are five Special Sites of Scientific Interest (SSSI) that can be found on the Bolton Abbey Estate. The first of these, and possibly the most important is Strid Wood, as the management prescription, which is lengthy, is primarily designed to continue forestry management operations without damaging or diminishing the exceptional wildlife habitats in the woodland. Woodland species of plants, lichen, butterflies, insects, birds (85 breeding species), mammals, reptiles, amphibians and bats have all been identified and their habitats recorded on maps of Strid Wood. See Appendix I. The protection of these creatures'

"Captain" the Forestry workhorse and his keeper Joe Dodson

Approved by the Craven Herald & Pioneer

natural environment is clearly part of the Estate's overall management plan. However, as it is difficult to keep all the natural environment out of bounds to people who also use this area for recreational activities like walking and fishing, the safeguarding of this Site of Special Scientific Interest can be problematic and visitors are always asked to keep dogs on a lead. The Estate has been able to solve this problem to some extent by redesigning footpaths to avoid places where protected species thrive. Some especially sensitive parts are fenced off. Locations of rare species of plants and birds are not identified in the Estate's guides for the public.

When maintenance work needs to be done in a protected woodland modern machinery can often accidentally damage the environment because it does not have the facility to move carefully in confined spaces. Woods that qualify as a Site of Special Scientific Interest deserve special treatment, so the Estate looked for an alternative way to carry out essential maintenance that was less intrusive.

Hambleton Quarry

A reef knoll at Cracoe

The solution came in the form of 'Captain' a shire horse who was bought to work with his keeper on thinning trees in Strid Wood. Captain could easily work in confined spaces and on slippery banks, and did far less damage to the ground – and its plant life, than a normal tractor. He was trained to haul felled timber from the woodland without snagging the tree trunks against growing trees, and played a major part in the Estate's forestry work until he retired in the 1990s. Outside working hours, Captain and Joe Dodson, his keeper, became firm favourites at many local fetes and agricultural shows where he would appear in full regalia, sometimes giving rides to children in his cart.

English Nature (now Natural England) have been particularly helpful to the Estate management team by assisting in the preservation of the trees in Strid Wood.

Paris quadrifolia is one of the strange, rare plants unusually found here as it normally only occurs in the eastern parts of Britain, and there are many rare species of lichen, some of which have been manually encouraged to flourish by transplanting to new host trees. Strid Wood is also the home, along with other broadleaved woodlands on the Estate, to squirrels. The grey squirrel is now the dominant species in the area, having ousted the indigenous population of red squirrels. Regular efforts are made to control the grey squirrel as it damages trees, and steals the eggs and young chicks of the woodlands birds. The grey squirrel is having a devastating impact on our song bird populations, definitely a top predator of farmland birds as confirmed by Professor Brown of Birkbeck, University of London. In areas of high squirrel density over 93% of small bird nests are devastated. Add the Sparrowhawk activity and it can result in 100% breeding failure and mean a loss of 85% of adult birds. At the moment there is a European research programme being undertaken which hopes to foster the re-introduction of the red squirrel into Britain and Ireland, and the removal of its rival grey cousin from northern Europe completely. The walk through Strid Wood to the Strid, along the carriageway (the Green trail), is the most popular one on the Estate as it is virtually on level ground all the way, through attractive woodland along the side of the river, with views as originally made by the 6th Duke still maintained, and produces the ultimate sight of the entire river gushing through a narrow gorge. At the end of the 18th century in fact, for these attractive footpaths and the carriage way in Strid Wood we have to thank a remarkable man, the Rev. William Carr, incumbent of Bolton Priory, but also the Duke's agent who laid out 30 miles of footpaths, both in Strid Wood and elsewhere, open to the public and with established seats and moss huts at strategic points near the river. These also opened up the natural wild life to the public. Legend has it that William, the 'Boy of Egremont' was drowned at the Strid in 1128 when he tried to jump from one side of the river to the other. When he jumped, his dog on a lead held back and William fell into the rushing water. His sorrowing mother, Alice de Romille is said to have founded the Priory as a result of this tragic accident but historians have discovered the boy's signature on a document after the alleged date of his 'death'. However, the Strid is a very dangerous place which has claimed the lives of some of those who have fallen in or tried to jump across the gap, although visitors are duly warned.

The second Site of Special Scientific Interest on the Estate is Hambleton Quarry. It was designated a SSSI in 1991 because it has a fine section of the marine carboniferous limestone found in the Craven Basin. The quarry which is close to the A59 road and lies beside Bolton Abbey railway station, consists of Asbian Draughton Limestone and Draughton Shale. The Draughton Shale has one of the best sections of Tiddeman's Breccia to be found in England and so the site is considered to be of national importance. Unfortunately, the quarried stone is unsuitable for roadstone and therefore the quarry is not in use at the present time. However, the railway line adjoining the site has been relaid, and a 3½ mile train service, partly steam, now runs as a tourist and enthusiasts attraction between Bolton Abbey and Embsay.

Cracoe Reef Knolls, between the village of Cracoe and Thorpe, have been designated the third Site of Special Scientific Interest because their limestone knolls have unusual flora, fauna and physiological features. There are several knolls in this area, and it is possible that the Estate bought Langerton Farm in the past because it would yield limestone from a knoll that lies within its boundaries. Because of its SSSI status quarrying of this limestone is now very unlikely, and the farm flourishes as a typical Yorkshire Dales farm, and also offers Bed and Breakfast to visitors.

The two moorlands, Barden Moor and Barden Fell have recently been added to the Sites of Special Scientific Interest.

English Nature with assistance from the Yorkshire Dales National Park and the Wharfedale Naturalists Society have recorded 85 species of breeding birds, 64 species of resident birds, 23 species of summer migrants, 14 species of winter migrants and 14 species of passage birds within the Estate boundary. The goshawk was listed as a passage bird in the survey but recently one or two pairs have been seen in one of the coniferous woods, and remarkably the

Top Left:
Great Spotted Woodpecker

Top Right:
Pied Flycatcher

Bottom Left:
Nuthatch

Bottom Right:
Kingfisher

By kind permission of the Yorkshire Dales National Park

Red Kites have also established themselves, and have successfully bred for the last two years. Other birds such as the barn owl are now rarely seen on the Estate. However, in the 1960s they were plentiful, with at least one pair in every field barn, and local people can remember how they used to swoop down on moving vehicles. The decline in numbers of the barn owl on the Estate is thought by some to have been caused by farmers transferring to silage production rather than continuing to make hay. However, experts have pointed to a shortage of their main food supply, field voles, which is probably caused by the increased number of sheep grazing on hill pastures.

Birdlife on the Estate can be seen in four main areas – the Wharfe Valley is characterised by meadows and woodlands where river and moorland birds can be seen. The species commonly found on the river banks are moorhens, oystercatchers, sandpipers, sand martins, dippers, goosanders, herons, kingfishers, wagtails and mallards. While the woodland and meadow birds include wood pigeons, nuthatches, rooks, jackdaws, kestrels, woodpeckers, owls, cuckoos, sparrow hawks, treecreepers, pheasants, woodcocks, wrens, tits, finches and warblers – Posforth Gill and Pickles Gill which make up the valley and hill sides are home to wagtails, wood pigeons, starlings, swallows, swifts, house martins, rooks, woodpeckers, curlews, lapwings, redstarts, bullfinches, buzzards, kestrels, sparrow hawks, tits, finches, fieldfares, partridges and pheasants – the moorlands which are situated mid estate on the western and eastern sides of the river provide a habitat for grouse, merlins, short eared owls, an occasional skylark, sparrow hawks, meadow pipits, snipes, redshanks, curlews, golden plovers, lapwings and dunlins.

It is interesting to note that a survey of wading birds by English Nature over Rylstone Fell and Embsay Moor in 1983 recorded the highest density of breeding waders in North Yorkshire and Durham. Specific species included golden plover, lapwing, dunlin, snipe, curlew, and redshank. This survey stressed the importance of flushes and damp areas for waders. Coincidentally, this is also recognised, and encouraged by the Estate, for grouse breeding as the newly born grouse require insects in the first weeks of their life which they can usually find in waterborn areas. Predators such as colonies of Lesser Black Backed gulls try to settle and breed on the moor above Upper Barden Reservoir but these are disturbed annually by Estate game keepers to try and prevent them settling as they feed on and can devastate young birds.

The biggest colony of gulls on the Estate are Black Headed gulls; they breed on the banks of the Upper Barden Reservoir in their hundreds. This expanse of water also provides a home for flocks of Canada and Greylag geese which breed on the moor and use the reservoir as a safety zone until the young can fly.

The moors also provide a home for a number of birds of prey including Short Eared Owls and Merlins. Merlins are surveyed every year and six or seven breeding pairs are regularly recorded.

The Estate is home to many species of butterflies with a recent English Nature survey recording 14 species. The butterfly which seems to be of greatest

Blackheaded Gull colony at Upper Barden Reservoir

interest is the Green Hairstreak, Callophrys Rubi. The Estate maintains this butterfly's natural habitat in this area which is covered in bilberry and heather. English Nature have recorded 13 species of mammals, 4 species of bats, 3 of reptiles and 3 species of amphibians. See Appendix 1. Amongst the mammals only two species of deer have been identified – the roe deer which is prevalent in most woodlands now, and the sika deer which is seen on the fringes of the Estate. All foxes are controlled by the Estate keepers as they frequent the moorland areas mainly and the positions of their regular dens or earths become known. Rabbits have become very numerous and now survive in the bottom of stone walls as well as burrows on the hill farms. Perhaps we have always assumed that rabbits have been plentiful in the Yorkshire Dales for countless generations, living in burrows along the riverside or in the rough grazing areas. However, it is interesting to learn that at Barden Tower, the hunting lodge originally associated with Skipton Castle, and the home of the 10th Lord Clifford, the "Shepherd Lord" (1485-1523), who enlarged it and created parkland for deer, also managed a large hillside area known as "Coney Warren" for rabbits. This became a great breeding ground and no doubt also provided a good supply of food in the winter months for his numerous staff at Barden Tower. Sadly, the brown hare has declined in numbers recently, but badgers remain numerous throughout the Estate. Some of the badgers have very distinctive setts in the old woodlands, and their lifestyle is left undisturbed.

The whereabouts of one rare plant – the Lady's Slipper Orchid – was kept secret. Mr Hey, the then Land Agent was one of the guardians enlisted to ensure its survival. On one occasion in the mid 1940s, the Duke asked his Land Agent to show the plant to a valued friend of his who would be coming up from London.

Mr Hey agreed, met the visitor at Leeds railway station, and took him in his car via a circuitous route that encompassed Lancashire and distant parts of Yorkshire. The final leg of the journey was organised so that the site was approached from Nidderdale, and the visitor must have been totally disorientated by the time he arrived at the secret location. The plant was duly photographed and admired before Mr Hey returned his visitor to Leeds railway station by following the route in reverse order. The guardian's mystery tour was helped by the absence of road signs on the roads which had yet to be replaced following the end of the Second World War.

One of the great experiences the Estate has to offer is to discover the early morning chorus of song birds in Strid Wood. During the spring time you would need to be hidden in the wood by 4.00 am, to listen as the song of the birds gradually builds up as the morning breaks. The obvious test then is to try and identify the unseen birds by their songs!

Living in the Wharfe valley can bring many surprises like the sudden appearance near the Priory one day of a white stork, of ospreys diving in the river at Barden on passage through the area, of geese flying northwards up the river, and while walking through Strid Wood to see dragonflies beside the water, the darting flight of a kingfisher and dippers regularly spaced feeding in the shallows.

Lady's Slipper Orchid

By kind permission of Stephen Morley for the National Trust

New arrivals to the Estate came in the 1970s, when a flock of goosanders came south from Scotland and took a fancy for fishing in the Wharfe and at Lower Barden Reservoir. They liked the place, stayed throughout the year, raised their young, and have been there all year round ever since.

As you look at wonderful landscapes which have been created by forestry, hill farming and wild life management all working together, now for two and a half centuries within the control and foresight of one family, we have much to be thankful for. Would those predecessors ever believe that seven generations later everybody would be welcome to come and enjoy this part of Wharfedale. People have moulded the landscape and now protect all its precious contours.

There has been a positive shift in the importance of certain areas on the Estate since the 1960s, when Nature Conservancy was only given a low priority. Nowadays the principles of nature conservation underpin much of the Estate's management plan, and it occupies a place of distinctive importance in the way this area is developed. So, the Estate continues its supportive dialogue with Natural England, which began with English Nature in 1983, regarding the identification of other habitats of particular conservation interest which may require special management practices to protect rare or threatened species.

This change would certainly have pleased the 11th Duke, as he always personally treasured the wildlife, and saw it as part of his social responsibilities to ensure that nature conservation was at the heart of the Estate's management culture. He was ahead of his time in wishing to actively protect fauna and flora on his land, and was keen to use the Estate to involve visitors in understanding how to preserve the natural environment for all to enjoy. Happily his personal interest has become fashionable and so Bolton Abbey will continue to be home to many species of animals, birds, insects, trees and flowers.

Green Hairstreak Butterfly

By approval of Richard Lewington of Butterfly Conservation Wareham

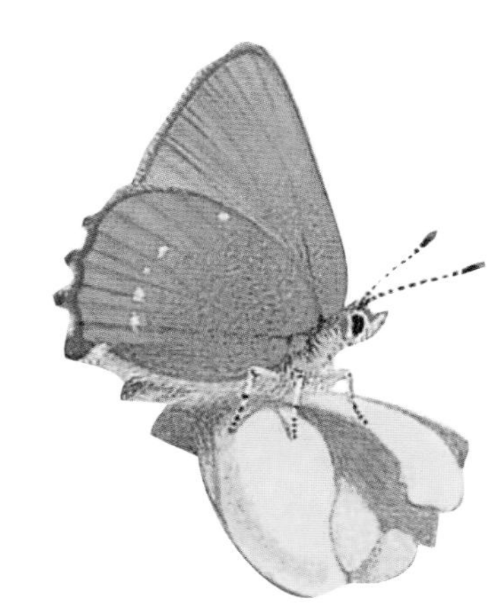

STEPPING OUT OF DOORS

The stepping stones at Bolton Abbey 1900

Tourism has grown dramatically over the last few decades to assume a place of major economic importance in national, regional and local economies. Alongside this development the opening up of what was once private land for public recreational use became a social imperative in the second half of the 20th century. As a result of these two trends tourism and public access to land are now two of the driving forces behind the management of the Bolton Abbey Estate.

Since the end of the Second World War landowners in England have come to realise that society at large had changed and that it was no longer considered appropriate for individuals to own, entirely for their own enjoyment, large tracts of land. The 11th Duke of Devonshire was one of the first to embrace the opportunities this change could offer as he firmly believed people were now entitled to share countryside previously enjoyed by wealthy landowners. At Chatsworth, one of his greatest pleasures in later life was to be able to look out of his study windows at the beauty of the park and see the countless numbers of people sharing its pleasure with him. This philosophy was also adopted at

Children enjoying the riverside

By kind permission of The Devonshire Arms Hotel

Bolton Abbey and the Estate began in the 1970s to actively encourage people to come and enjoy a day out in the country.

Nowadays the habit of spending time in the country is part of many people's weekend programme, and Bolton Abbey have responded to this trend by providing an original outdoor experience which tries to cater for a wide variety of leisure pursuits. Bolton Abbey is also ideally situated to serve as the "country retreat" for those who live in the large conurbations of Leeds, Bradford, Harrogate and Halifax which are all within one hour's drive of the Estate. So when 80% of this island's population live in cities or towns, it is increasingly likely that people will want to spend some of their leisure time in the country. How this desire is catered for and managed so that the countryside is not adversely affected is an everyday concern at Bolton Abbey, as the Estate has much to preserve and protect in terms of ancient buildings, wildlife habitats and farming income.

Bolton Abbey is now a place for all seasons. The name can uplift the spirit of thousands of visitors as the Estate in mid-Wharfedale is a place for recreation at any time of the year.

In winter walkers are seen trudging through the Valley of Desolation on their way to Simon's Seat.

Spring arrives and puts a sparkle on the river and

The Cavendish Pavilion, on the riverside at Sandholme car park

brings out the bluebells and other wild flowers to attract people into Strid Wood.

Summer offers the prospect of picnics on the river bank or a snack or meal in the Cavendish Pavilion, and in late summer the two moorlands show off their heather in a blaze of colour.

Autumn brings a variety of colour from the woodlands and fishermen are keen to enjoy the trout season before it finishes at the end of September. Not only the fishing but they will enjoy the wonderful variety of bird life on the riverside.

But tourism is not a new phenomenon in Wharfedale, as visitors started coming to Bolton Abbey when the 6th Duke of Devonshire gave access to the Strid and surrounding woodland in the early 1800s which allowed the public to see this natural phenomenon for the first time. The popularity of this attraction soon grew so paths were created and a carriageway constructed so that horse drawn wagonettes could ferry people to the Strid. Additional access routes soon followed opening up the riverside, the Valley of Desolation and the eastern moor to Simon's Seat. Permission to visit these places was given to visitors when they bought a 6d ticket, and to-day they remain very popular and the route to Simon's Seat is covered in the Open Access Agreement for Barden Fell.

The influx of visitors encouraged local residents to open up their cottages as tearooms, and so the first economic benefits of tourism were felt on the Estate. Extending the main railway line from the main line at Skipton to Bolton Abbey in the late 1800s resulted in a further increase in tourists, and such was visitor pressure at this time that the Estate had to consider what strategies could be put in place for the public to be properly accommodated. The Duke decided that refreshments needed to be concentrated in one place, and so cottage tearooms were closed down, and the Cavendish Pavilion near the entrance to Strid Wood by the river at Sandholme was built. The Pavilion with its enticing menu of light meals and afternoon teas was an instant success. This had been very successfully run as a major refreshment venue by the Tipling and Rogers families until 2006 when the Estate took the business in hand. The Devonshire Arms Hotel also benefited from the increased number of tourists as it was ideally situated being halfway between the station and Bolton Abbey village. So by the mid 1800s tourism had already made an impact on those who lived and worked on the Estate.

Internal view of The Pantry opened in 2002

The level of Estate involvement with public access remained stable until the post second world war period when issues of land ownership and usage became part of the wider political agenda. The first change came in the 1960s with the National Parks and Access to the Countryside Act 1949 which gave powers to the County Councils to seek land for public access and in due course the West Riding County Council concentrated on the Estate's moorlands. The agent at this time, Ernest Hey, did all he could to divert their attention from this issue until the Duke, fully understanding where his and the public interest lay, agreed to increase access on to the Estate moorland. This comprised open access by people on foot on 13,500 acres of the Estate's moorlands throughout the year for a period of 50 years.

Working with the County Council officers, the Duke agreed a list of controls and exemptions that allowed the Estate to maintain its traditional role as an agricultural country estate. For example, grouse management and shooting days were preserved, and sheep grazing rights would continue. It was also agreed, from the public's point of view, that no vehicles, no dogs, no fires, no horses, no access on shooting days would be allowed on this land; that walkers would be encouraged to keep to the main signposted routes, and that compensation would be paid to the Estate for any damage to ancient buildings or the land caused by the public. In order to help protect the Estate's agricultural interest the Yorkshire Dales National Park took on some of the custodial duties that would ensure that public access did not bring with it damage to the land and ancient buildings on the Estate. The National Park supplied maps at all the public access points, recruited a Warden and several voluntary Wardens to patrol the area and be available to help the public. This agreement has been extremely successful because of the close co-operation between the staff of both the Estate and the Yorkshire Dales National Park.

The opening up of the moorland areas provided several miles of good hill walking which proved to be extremely popular. In spite of the increased use of the land very little damage was done to the Estate. This was largely thanks to the Estate game keepers and to the efficient public relations exercise carried out by the National Park wardens to help the visitors enjoy the countryside peacefully. A length of footpath was even substantially repaired with stone near Simon's Seat by the Yorkshire Dales National Park. On one particular day, a Warden stopped and questioned the driver of an unusual Bentley car which had driven onto the moor. The passenger, the Duke, got out of his car, and thanked the Warden for doing his duty so correctly, and told him that he would be driving down off the moor directly.

However, by the late 1960s the supremacy of the car as the preferred method of transport and the public desire for increased access to open country in England, meant that the Estate had to re-assess its tourist policy and provision. The Duke and his Land Agent examined the range and quality of visitor amenities at Bolton Abbey, and measured these against those offered on similar estates. Many landowners were providing additional public attractions such as wildlife parks or children's farms which were very popular. However, despite the obvious popularity of these ventures at other small country estates, it was decided to go against the trend and rely solely on the natural attractiveness of the country as the magnet with which to secure a healthy number of visitors. The philosophy behind this decision was to encourage an enjoyment of the Estate for the quality of its natural beauty, and to make this the centrepiece of its marketing strategy when promoting it to the outside world.

Starting from this basis, the Estate management team devised a plan that would ensure that the land was kept in pristine condition and that all visitor amenities were to a high standard. Innovative management practices adopted by the Estate meant that tourism strategies were closely linked to the nature conservation and wildlife programmes which ensured that the natural environment was enhanced. This, of course, led to an unique visitor experience, which proved to be extremely popular.

The first strategy in the new tourism policy started in the 1970s when the Estate devoted a great deal of effort to improving the access for visitors. All the footpaths in Strid Wood were regraded and resurfaced. The 4 miles of riverside footpaths between Bolton Bridge and Barden Bridge were widened, and special gates installed particularly for dogs so that they could walk through and their owners were not expected to lift them over a fence. The Estate Office received many congratulatory letters from happy dog owners! In 2005 the dog gates and also the stiles were removed and new gates positioned so that these popular riverside routes were accessible to a wider population; young families, people with push chairs, and people with walking difficulties.

However, Estate provision for two significant sections of the community had not yet been achieved so in the 1980s plans were drawn up to assist the elderly and the disabled to enjoy the countryside more easily. From market research that the Estate team undertook they learnt that many visitors to the Priory and the riverside at the Cavendish Pavilion were elderly people and those with mobility problems. On inspection it became obvious that because the land had an easy gradient in these places more could be done to help these visitors. The Estate sought specialist advice from the Field Fare Trust and plans were developed after this consultation that opened up these areas to wheelchair access. It was straightforward to make all the stiles into gateways which had closing springs to keep cattle and sheep in the fields, while allowing wheelchairs through. The footpaths that could be used by disabled people were extended and an information campaign devised so that these special facilities were widely publicised. It soon became clear that some visitors would find it easier to visit the Estate if on-site wheelchairs were available to them. So 4 electric scooters and 2 wheelchairs were obtained and were offered for hire free of charge or on a voluntary donation at 2 locations; firstly, in Bolton Abbey village giving accesses to the Priory and riverside, and secondly at the Cavendish Pavilion where visitors could go to see the Strid.

Because there is a five mile stretch of river that is easily accessible Bolton Abbey is a very popular year round attraction and, for this reason, one of the major

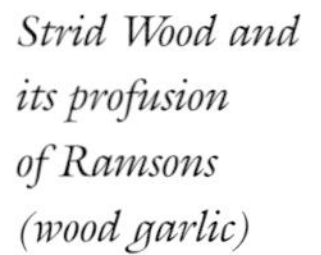

Strid Wood and its profusion of Ramsons (wood garlic)

concerns when considering how to ensure that the public enjoy the area is the positioning of car parks. This can be a difficult decision to make because on the one hand car parks have to be conveniently situated near the point of attraction or visitor amenities, while at the same time not detracting from the natural beauty of the countryside. In the case of Bolton Abbey four visitor locations with parking facilities have been carefully planned in different areas that receive the most visitors. Each of these areas have distinctive features and their individual identities are clearly marketed to encourage people who want to enjoy the same kind of activities or atmosphere to use a particular part of the Estate. So the first location is found in Bolton Abbey where visitors can enjoy the village amenities. This part of the Estate is ideal for families with children or elderly visitors who like a leisurely walk down to the river, a picnic or to visit the Priory Church.

Sandholme beside the river is the site of the Estate's most popular area, heavily used by families with children who come to enjoy playing in the water where the river is especially safe. This part of the Estate is ideal for those who want to spend the whole day outside in the country. It is also the best point of access for disabled visitors as the riverside walks here are flat and the paths remain in good condition even after wet weather. There is also a wide variety of visitor amenities here housed in the Cavendish Pavilion and adjoining buildings; these include a gift shop, café, restaurant, information and lavatories. Parking is well screened and does not spoil the view of the valley.

Access to the north end of Strid Wood also has parking facilities, complete with lavatories and a new built gift shop with interpretation of the local interests in nature and wildlife, opened recently in 2005. This stone building is particularly designed to reflect the surrounding environment of Strid Wood.

There is a further parking area at Barden Bridge just beyond the northern end of Strid Wood. The pleasant grass field has no shop, lavatories or tearoom, but this area appeals to walkers who want to leave their cars safely before taking long distance walks on the hills, moors or riverside. This is open during the summer months, but all the others are open throughout the year together with their gift shops.

In the 1970s it was decided that to improve visitor experience the Estate's principal car parks should be manned so that everyone received a proper welcome. Visitors receive, with their ticket, a leaflet which describes the facilities, places of interest on the Estate, and in the case of dog owners, a bag to encourage people to dispose of animal waste responsibly. Like any well used area with in excess of 500,000 visitors a year litter can be a real headache for the Estate maintenance staff. The Cavendish family are obviously keen that Bolton Abbey should always be looking at its best whenever anyone visits, so litter clearance is given a high priority. Recently, the Estate has become involved in a litter recycling initiative and visitors are encouraged to dispose of unwanted items in an environmentally friendly way. Today the Estate collects over 200 tonnes of litter each year. The grounds of the Estate that are open to the public do require constant attention to keep them clean and tidy, and the Grounds Maintenance Department of seven devoted men attend to this. Experience

People picnicking at the riverside in Sandholme Car Park

Cavendish Pavilion

over the years has shown Robert Dixon, the Head of Department, what is necessary at what time of the year and what machinery or equipment is essential. Grass cutting, particularly the car parks, involves several acres, the footpaths are several miles long, and all litter has to be collected. Additional work now contracted out includes the two hotels, the Priory graveyard, the Tea rooms, Village Hall, Barden Tower and some of these require hanging baskets, seasonal plants for tubs or bedding out, and a regular contact with the hotel chefs is necessary to manage their vegetable gardens. Work over the years seems to have grown and now includes maintenance of the roadside verges between Bolton Bridge and the entrance to the Cavendish Pavilion.

In the modern world Bolton Abbey has to market its attractions to secure its visitor numbers in an increasingly competitive tourist environment. Marketing is central to the success of the Estate as a tourist destination and is grounded in detailed information about the visitor profile for Bolton Abbey. Leaflets are produced describing all the attractions, including farmhouses where Bed and Breakfast and local accommodation is available, and all information is displayed now on a website. Detailed surveys are commissioned every 5 years or so that help to identify the way in which the Estate is perceived and used by its visitors. This data is then used to make sure that the Estate is providing the kind of information that will attract visitors to the area and enhance their experience when visiting. In addition the Estate has its own website, produces a major promotional leaflet which is widely distributed on a regional, national and international basis. However, the marketing strategy must ensure that those who come to visit understand the special nature of the place so are willing to help safeguard the environment as well as enjoy their time here. It is considered very important that visitors receive a welcome when arriving at Bolton Abbey so all car parks are manned and the new village shop, positioned in the main car park does this with information on personally designed placards, with leaflets describing the various attractions and interests and staff available to help with all general information.

The former village shop and Post Office has been sensitively converted into a book shop, concentrating on old books, known as the Grove Rare Book shop managed by Andrew Sharpe formerly of Ilkley.

In general as far as access to private land is concerned the Countryside and Rights of Way Act 2000 came into operation in this area in 2005. Happily it did not override the Access Agreement of Barden Moor and Barden Fell of 1968, but the Estate was consulted extensively as open access had been provided here for many years. Although the Estate does make a charge for access, it has been deemed necessary to generate income to offset the cost of maintaining this particular part of Wharfedale and for providing the information and facilities for visitors. Hopefully this will also help to present and protect this area for future generations.

Visitor numbers to Bolton Abbey fluctuate from year to year with the area being particularly heavily used at the weekends and in the school holidays. Meeting the demands of such a regular influx of people as well as keeping the Estate running as an agricultural and commercial enterprise and protecting its environmental importance is a complex balancing act. Today, many interests and organisations share in helping the Estate and happily it can count on positive support from the Tourist Board, Regional Development Agencies and, of course, those who come to enjoy its special atmosphere.

FUTURE

The Devonshire family have owned the Bolton Abbey Estate for over 250 years, and the length of their tenure has meant that they have been able to see many of their plans come to fruition. However, like many other country estates, Bolton Abbey faces an uncertain future and its chances of survival in the modern world are dependent on the foundations that have been laid to ensure it is managed and preserved for the Cavendish family and future generations to enjoy. Its financial security has been greatly helped by the fact that the greater part of the Trustees of the Chatsworth Settlement's Bolton Abbey Estate has been designated as heritage property which means that it is exempt from Capital Transfer Tax.

As a condition of this tax exemption the Trustees prepared a Landscape, Conservation and Recreation plan for the Estate in consultation with the Countryside Agency – acting on behalf of the Capital Taxes Office. This plan will preserve the area's essential landscape features and that will ensure it continues to provide extensive recreational facilities for its many visitors. The Estate has a long tradition of land management for multiple use, with careful attention to quality and conservation, so it will be able to build on this experience to maintain this beautiful part of Wharfedale and hopefully cope with any future increase in visitor numbers.

Agricultural Acts always have an impact on the management of country estates, and in some instances, can alter the direction of their development. The recent political interest in the countryside which has been one of the dominant themes of the early part of this century, will hopefully lead to legislation that will support farming, forestry, heritage property and wildlife. This kind of political and social reform would be enormously helpful to the Bolton Abbey Estate as it tries to maintain a traditional country life at a time when the farming community in the Yorkshire Dales find it increasingly difficult to make a living from the land. At the moment, for instance, the declining price of milk offered to dairy farmers needs urgent reassessment, as low prices force farmers out of business and off the land. A change in the milk marketing policy could reverse this trend and encourage hill farms to flourish, as the farmers do, after all, cherish and maintain in good heart the much enjoyed countryside.

Village life in the parishes also needs protecting by central government instigating a housing policy that provides rural communities with better and more affordable housing. The situation needs to change so that retired tenant farmers, farm workers and associates can continue to live in the rural areas or villages where they have spent most of their lives. As rural housing is so expensive, they have, at the moment to live elsewhere and this can cause problems as they become lonely and isolated from their support networks. An increase in the availability of rented housing may be the practical solution, and the support of landowners who would be willing to

On a school visit children enjoy a close look at a Brown Trout

By kind approval of the Craven Herald & Pioneer

provide this type of accommodation for the use of the young people who work on their estates as well as those in retirement could be the answer.

Farming under the Common Agricultural Policy is directed towards less dependency on government support and more on direct marketing and the needs of society. This is indeed welcome and should help the small family farm at Bolton Abbey, but more concrete assistance is required to ensure the survival of local food production and quality farming in this area. The Country Landowners and Rural Business Association also states that "local food has, after all, a lower carbon footprint than food that has been transported halfway across the planet, and Britain has some of the highest animal welfare standards in the world. Hence buying local food should ensure that there is a future for farming", ….. particularly here in the Yorkshire Dales! Several organisations such as Sustainable Farming and Food Strategy, Food Partnerships, and Framework for Change are all trying to support these kinds of initiatives. Perhaps all these organisations will work together to produce a set of common objectives which will positively help the small family farmer.

An appreciation of the fact that farming and forestry help form the landscape that visitors want to enjoy is becoming recognised. This is especially the case at Bolton Abbey where hill sheep farming and game management have had a significant impact on the landscape increasing its natural beauty. The "real star" of the show, and the reason why Bolton Abbey is so popular is the distinctive landscape characterised by riverside walks which take you through ancient forests and provide dramatic views of upland moorland. Introducing children and adults to country life is a special interest of the Duke and Duchess who have founded the Devonshire Educational Trust which has the express purpose of promoting education and encouraging an understanding of rural issues and concerns.

The Estate has become more outward looking over the past 30 years, and now consults with a wide range of organisations. For instance, English Heritage, Natural England, the Yorkshire Dales National Park Authority, the Tourist Board, DEFRA and the Country Landowners Business Association all help to maintain and conserve this area's landscape, workforce, heritage and wildlife. Its outside contacts are wide ranging and encompass organisations as diverse as the Council for the Protection of Rural England, the British Christmas Tree Growers Association, Game Conservancy, Meteorological Office, the British Deer Society and the Agricultural Wages Board.

The 12th Duke and Duchess of Devonshire with their son Lord Burlington

By kind permission of the Devonshire Collection, Chatsworth

It is everybody's wish, I believe, that the Estate will remain secure in the years to come, and that it will continue to attract support, when necessary, from interested parties. The Devonshire family have built strong ties with the local community, and actively seek to share the Estate with those who live and work there but most generously with members of the public who visit Bolton Abbey. The family believe that all those who enjoy the Estate are stakeholders in the drive to secure it for future generations to enjoy. By opening the Estate to the public the Duke has gained widespread support which should help to protect the landscape and wildlife. However, one of the strengths of the Bolton Abbey Estate, and to my mind, the reason why it has survived over the last 30 years, is that it has been in the hands of one family of clear vision, for over two and a half centuries. This has given the Estate a secure foundation from which to develop and plan for the future, and we are enormously grateful for the 11th Duke of Devonshire's decision that the family interest in Bolton Abbey should be secured.

The success of this Estate has undoubtedly been created by the owners, their staff and every individual employee who has worked for the Dukes over the years. Their devotion to duty and understanding and enjoyment of their contribution to the maintenance and development of this Yorkshire Dales Estate has been an essential part of its survival. They have enjoyed being employed at Bolton Abbey, and many have long service running to over 40 years, and in two cases over 50 years. Some of them choose to live in tied Estate accommodation and then move elsewhere on retirement. Residential property available for letting is snapped up, and house prices in villages adjacent to the Estate have risen sharply over the last 10 years. Barn conversions are much sought after. Visitor numbers continue to increase, and the Estate attracts regular media attention. All these factors seem to indicate that the management plan for the Bolton Abbey Estate is working, and that secure foundations for its future are in place. So, Bolton Abbey in 2006, I believe, is achieving that most difficult of balancing acts – combining the traditions of a medieval agricultural estate with being one of the premier visitor attractions in Yorkshire!

In an uncertain world no one can be sure about the future of the Cavendish family and their possessions. Dukes have possibly become a rare and endangered species, and although the succession to the Devonshire Dukedom seems assured, there is no certainty about the long-term tenure of the Bolton Abbey Estate.

But the Dukes of Devonshire have all shown their very keen family interests in those who live and work on their Yorkshire Dales Estate in preserving its special features, maintaining and substantially improving it, and their ability to manipulate changes and provide interest in sharing substantial parts of it with members of the public. This, hopefully, should ensure it is set to survive into at least another century.

Currently information on the Estate is available on the website www.boltonabbey.com

Epilogue

"The Spirit of Bolton Abbey"

"Life for many has the unalloyed verve of an undressed lettuce.

The camera of their minds does not dwell on the landing of a wild trout from the Wharfe, or the downing of malt whiskies in the Duke's bar after a day among the pheasants and woodcock.

Their noses do not twitch at the smell of pine from the forester's fire, or of a wet moor in August.

They do not feel the banter of a morning shoot.

They do not hear the call of a curlew in the wild or splash through dew in the fresh of an early morning sun.

They do not care that talons strike on defenceless prey, nor catch the smell of raw milk in concrete shippons.

They do not see the dance of hares in display or the blue flash of a kingfisher's flight.

They do not care for the chase, or the sweat of a horse or the bleat of a new born lamb.

They do not hear the ethereal sounds of the choir in the church or the noontide toll of the Angelus bell.

They do not hear the laughter of children having fun or share the hiker's dream of a view from the top. They do not stop and listen to the silence.

I say may it long continue, in an island crammed tighter with people than tadpoles in a schoolboy's jar. It is essential that we live and let live. We must live a great deal, in fact to the fullest extent wherever possible, and without the puritanical constraints that some would impose as part of their "politically correct agenda".

We should never question the need to drink a bottle of claret single handed, but do demand that "expert" science and spin doctored opinion takes second place to plain common sense and personal liberty.

If you feel the same, then the spirit of Bolton Abbey has not failed you."

John Sheard on the occasion of his retirement party as Land Agent for the Bolton Abbey Estate on 28th August 1998.

Appendix I
Strid Wood – a site of special scientific interest

The Strid Wood and Oak Pasture designated as a site of special Scientific Interest in 1985 lie in the middle of the Bolton Abbey Estate. The Strid Woods lie either side of the River Wharfe which bisects the Estate virtually in half in a north south direction. The Oak Wood Pasture at Laund lies on a shelf of agricultural land on the east bank of the river between Strid Wood and the moors. Together these areas total some 59 hectares.

Description

Strid Wood contains the largest area of acidic oak woodland and the best remnant of oak wood pasture in the Yorkshire Dales National Park. The wood is set astride the River Wharfe, which here runs through a deep steep-sided valley cut into Millstone Grit and Carboniferous Limestone.

The northeast side of the valley supports oak forest with a largely acidic ground flora of Woodrush (*Luzula sylvatica*), Bilbery (*Vaccinium myrtillus*), wavy hair grass (*Deschampsia flexuosa*), and several species of fern. Holly (*Ilex aquifolium*), Birch (*Betula pubescens*) and Hazel (*Corylus avellana*) are also present as well as a number of both self-sown and planted Beech and Sycamore. There are occasional flushes where the limestone influence is more strongly felt, and here the canopy comprises Elm (*Ulmus glabra*) and Alder (*Alnus glutinosa*), with a ground flora containing such species as opposite-leaved Golden-saxifrage (*Chrysosplenium oppositifolium*), Wood melick (*Melica uniflora*) and Mountain melick (*M. nutans*). Above the road, there is an area of relict wood pasture in which old pollards of Oak, Holly and Birch are growing amongst bracken and acid grassland.

The southwest bank has been much altered by forestry practice. The Native Oak (*Quercus petraea*) and Ash (*Fraxinus excelsior*) are accompanied by plantations of Beech (*Fagus sylvatica*), Sycamore (*Acer pseudoplatanus*), Poplar (*Populus*) and conifers such as Larch and Douglas Fir. The very edge of the river however remains largely natural, with Elm and Alders. Soil conditions on this side of the valley appear less acidic, and the ground flora is rich, with stands of Dog's mercury (*Mercuarialis perennis*), Ramsons (*Allium ursinum*) Sanicle (*Sanicula europaea*) and Sweet woodruff (*Asperula odoratum*). The uncommon yellow Star of Bethlehem (*Gagea lutea*) is found here.

The wood is valued by naturalists for its important populations of many groups of plants and animals. There is a rich bryophyte flora, several species being rare or very local in distribution including Dicranum montanum, Cinclidotus mucronatus, Fissidens rufulus, Nowellia curvifolia and Sphagnum Quinquefarium. A wide variety of fungi occur, two species Coprinus subpurpureus and Deconica rhombispora, being first British records. Woodland management by selective felling rather

APPENDIX I (CONTINUED)

than clear felling has ensured a continuity of tree cover, and has favoured the growth of a rich lichen flora: indeed Strid Wood is considered one of the best lichen woods in Yorkshire. Amongst the most notable species recorded are Arthonia didyma, Thelotrema lepadinum, Cladonia parasitica and Endocarpon pusillum. The wood is also noted for the occurrence of the local molluscs Acanthinula lamellata and Lauria anglica.

Strid Wood General

The Estate policy will be one of support for the SSSI whilst at the same time allowing public access. The Estate agrees to maintain the woodland to preserve the specified locations and species detailed in the plan and its appendix. It also agrees to maintain the general acidic oak woodland aspect, particularly on the east bank with the emphasis there of a gradual strengthening of the oak content. On the west bank the existing proportions of species mix to be retained.

It is agreed that timber, especially oak, may be removed from the woodlands under the agreed plan and used either on the Estate or sold to contribute towards the cost of maintaining the woodland.

The control of pests (e.g., foxes, rabbits, mink, grey squirrels) is to continue to be the Estate's responsibility and the exercise of fishing rights on the river is to continue as at present.

This document is to be used as the agreed management policy by the Estate, NCC and Forestry Commission. It is to be subject to review and revision every five years to coincide with the Forestry Commission Plan of Operations revision. During the final five years all sides will carefully monitor progress to avoid misunderstandings and achieve the best results.

THE BOLTON ABBEY ESTATE
BIRDS

Key:		
	(B)	Breeding bird
	R	Resident
	S	Summer migrant
	W	Winter migrant
	P	Passage (Spring or Autumn migration)

(B)	R	Little Grebe
(B)	R	Great Crested Grebe
		Grey Heron
	P	Greylag Goose
(B)	R	Canada Goose
	W	Barnacle Goose
	P	Shelduck
	W	Widgeon
(B)	R	Teal
(B)	R	Mallard
	W	Shoveller
	W	Pochard
(B)	R	Tufted Duck
	W	Goldeneye
(B)	R	Goosander
	W	Hen Harrier
	P	Goshawk
(B)	R	Sparrowhawk
	P	Buzzard
	W	Roughlegged Buzzard
	P	Golden Eagle
	P	Osprey

		Barn Owl
(B)	R	Little Owl
(B)	R	Tawny Owl
(B)	R	Short-eared Owl
(B)	S	Swift
(B)	S	Sandmartin
(B)	S	Swallow
(B)	S	House Martin
(B)	R	Kingfisher
(B)	R	Green Woodpecker
(B)	R	Great Spotted Woodpecker
		Lesser Spotted Woodpecker
(B)	S	Skylark
		Tree Pipit
(B)	R	Meadow Pipit
(B)	S	Yellow Wagtail
(B)	R	Grey Wagtail
(B)	R	Pied Wagtail
	P	White Wagtail

(B) R Kestrel
(B) S Merlin
P Hobby
P Peregrine

(B) R Red Grouse
R Red-legged Partridge
(B) R Grey Partridge
(B) R Pheasant

(B) R Moorhen
(B) R Coot
(B) S Oystercatcher
P Little Ringed Plover
P Ringed Plover
(B) S Golden Plover
(B) R Lapwing
(B) S Dunlin
(B) R Snipe
(B) R Woodcock
P Whimbrel
(B) S Curlew
(B) S Redshank
P Greenshank
(B) S Common Sandpiper
(B) R Black-headed Gull
(B) R Lesser Black-backed Gull
(B) R Stock Dove
(B) R Wood pigeon
(B) R Collared Dove
(B) S Cuckoo

(B) R Blue Tit
(B) R Great Tit
(B) R Nuthatch
(B) R Tree Creeper
(B) R Jay

(B) R Magpie
(B) R Jackdaw
(B) R Rook
(B) R Carrion Crow
P Raven

(B) R Dipper

(B) R Wren
(B) R Dunnock
(B) R Robin
(B) S Whinchat
W Stonechat

(B) S Ring Ouzel
(B) R Blackbird
W Fieldfare
(B) R Song Thrush
W Mistle Thrush
W Redwing

(B) S Lesser Whitethroat
S Whitethroat
(B) S Garden Warbler
(B) S Chiffchaff
(B) S Willow Warbler
(B) R Goldcrest
(B) S Spotted Flycatcher
(B) S Pied Flycatcher

(B) R Long-tailed Tit
(B) R Marsh Tit
(B) R Willow Tit
(B) R Coal Tit

(B) R Starling
(B) R House Sparrow
(B) R Chaffinch
W Brambling
(B) R Greenfinch
(B) R Goldfinch
W Siskin
(B) R Linnet
(B) R Twite
(B) R Redpoll
(B) R Crossbill
(B) R Bullfinch
W Snow Bunting
(B) R Yellow Hammer
(B) R Reed Bunting

This information has been supplied from records held by the Yorkshire Dales National Park and the Wharfedale Naturalist Trust.

OTHER SPECIES

BUTTERFLIES

Large Skipper
Large White
Green Veined White
Orange Tip
Small White
Small Copper
Green Hairstreak
Common Blue
Small Tortoiseshell
Red Admiral
Peacock
Small Heath
Meadow Brown
Wall Brown

REPTILES

Adder
Slow Worm
Common Lizard

AMPHIBIANS

Frogs
Toads
Newts

MAMMALS

Roe Deer - most woodlands on the Estate contain Roe Deer
Sika Deer - have been seen on the fringes of the Estate
Fox
Badger
Stoat
Weasel
Feral Mink
Brown Hare
Rabbit
Grey Squirrel
Mole
Brown Rat

Plus several species of mice, voles and shrew

BATS

Although identification of bats can only be done accurately in the hand, several different species of bat have been seen and are thought to include:

Noctule
Pipistrelle
Brown Long-eared
Daubentons

This information has been supplied from records held by the Yorkshire Dales National Park and the Wharfedale Naturalist Trust.

Appendix II
The Valley of Desolation

A totally new and ambitious development scheme has been adequately researched by Roy Lingard and Trevor Nash to renovate the Valley of Desolation as an educational trail giving people a greater understanding of the countryside.

This will illustrate how the landscape has evolved over the years and it is hoped that people will be encouraged to gain a deeper insight into the countryside and mankind's influence upon it.

Establishing woodlands is a long term project covering many decades, and this is being emphasised to the general public as the woodlands develop.

The aims of the trail are to interpret the following sequence of events.

Climate and succession of tree species

The purpose of the Valley of Desolation Nature trail is to illustrate the changes in this country over the last 25,000 years or so. Over the last 2,000,000 years it is estimated that there have been approximately 20 Ice Ages. The last one ended some 11,000 years ago and we are currently in an interglacial period of relative warmth.

10,000 years ago the climate began to warm and the ice retreat. The succession of tree species, (from pollen records) during the various periods or phases since the last Ice Age were as follows:

With the retreat of the glaciers the climate was dry and cold; the vegetation cover was Arctic tundra with willow scrub, dwarf birch, juniper and vaccinium.

The Boreal stage, 8,000-5,500 BC the early stages of this period saw the Northern progression of great numbers of birch following behind the retreating ice cap.

Not far behind came Scots pine (though much less dominant than birch) with some hazel, oak, elm and alder. Scots pine continued its spread northward and during the later Boreal stage started to become dominant over birch. Pine and birch woods spread to higher elevations and colonised the uplands.

About 6,000 BC – the climate continued to become milder. Pine continued its spread northward, beginning to dominate the birch. In most of England the birch gave way before pine, but the former kept its dominance in Wales, Scotland and Northern Ireland.

In the mid-Boreal centuries oak and elm also made a slow advance from small bridgeheads established in the pre-Boreal phase, but remaining far below the level of pine. For quite a time large parts of the British

Isles were covered in pine forests. Hazel reached its maximum distribution during the early Boreal period, spreading to the extreme north of Scotland.

Atlantic phase, 5500-2500 BC – an increase in moisture and a sustained highter temperature mark the Atlantic phase. This period saw an important change in the vegetation of the British Isles with broadleaf woodlands increasing until they became dominant. During this period deciduous summer forests were established. Elm Pedunculate and Sessile oak spread widely bringing with them some small-leaved lime, which became common in certain localities.

With the exception of heathlands, limestone and wetter areas, oak became the dominant tree of the Atlantic phase woodlands and remained so at lower altitudes in most of England, Wales, Ireland and Southern Scotland. Pine and birchwoods retain their dominance in the more upland areas and Northern Scotland. Elm was much more frequent than it became in historic times.

Later alder began to succeed pine, remaining important until historic times. There are also traces of ash in Atlantic times, but it increased after this period. *During this period over 70% of the British land surface was cloaked in woodlands*.

Sub-Boreal Phase 2000 BC-700BC the climate becomes drier but remains mild. Beech spreads to Southwest England and possibly Wales, becoming the dominant tree on chalk uplands. On the limestone areas ash and yew were the dominant species.

Sub Atlantic phase, approximately 700-550 BC – the weather becomes wetter and cooler. With this change, precipitation is greater than evaporation and vast swamps and marshes formed, beginning to overwhelm many of the birch and pine forests, which were the climax vegetation of highland Britain. In this way the peat bogs of Northern England and on a larger scale in Scotland began to take shape. Neolithic man began early forest clearances.

From 550 BC the climate fluctuated relatively rapidly in geological terms, with a warm period between 400-1200 AD, (when vineyards were cultivated in southern England). This was followed by cold stormy weather during 1200 and 1300 AD. These fluctuations continue to the present day.

This period saw an increasing destruction of forests, until finally the wooded area in Britain amounted to *only 6% of the land area at the start of the 20th century.*

Our grateful thanks are enthusiastically given to Roy Lingard and Trevor Nash for their detailed research and planning of the trail, to the following who gave financial support:

Yorkshire Dales Millennium Trust

Yorventure

The Forestry Commission

English Nature

And the following who undertook the contract work:

Nigel Davison and Mark Hawkins – Fencing

Bob Middleton – Footpath Construction

Gary Priestnall – Computer Simulation

Peter Drew – Printing of the Interpretive Panel

Production and Artwork of Interpretive Panel – Roy Lingard.

The Cavendish Family Tree

Bolton Abbey Estate passed to The Cavendish family through the marriage of Lady Charlotte Boyle to William Cavendish, who became the 4th Duke of Devonshire in 1755.

Lady Charlotte's ancestors were the Lords of Skipton.

1720-1764
William Cavendish
4th Duke of Devonshire
Started serious grouse shooting from Bolton Abbey. Built Rocking Hall (then known as Rocking House) as a shooting Lodge.
≈
1731 - 1754
Lady Charlotte Boyle
dau. of the 4th Earl of Cork and 3rd Earl of Burlington; estates in Yorkshire and Ireland, Chiswick House, Burlington House.

1748-1811
William Cavendish
5th Duke of Devonshire
≈
1757-1806 (1) Lady Georgiana Spencer
dau. of the 1st Earl Spencer
1757-1824 (2) Lady Elizabeth Foster (née Hervey)

1754-1834
Lord George Cavendish
1st Earl of Burlington (2nd creation)
≈
1760-1835 Lady Elizabeth Compton

1790-1858
William Spencer Cavendish
6th Duke of Devonshire
The Bachelor Duke. At 21 he inherited 8 houses and 200,000 acres of land. Employed Sir Joseph Paxton who designed the Crystal Palace to alter and extend Bolton Hall.

1783-1858
Lady Georgiana Cavendish
≈
1773-1848
George Howard

1783-1812
William Cavendish
Killed in carriage accident
≈
-d.1863
Hon. Louisa O'Callaghan

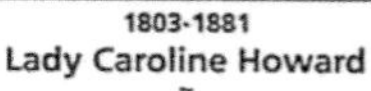

1803-1881
Lady Caroline Howard
≈
1798-1851
Rt. Hon. William Lascelles
Son of the 2nd Earl of Harewood

1838-1920
Emma Lascelles
≈
1838-1891
Lord Edward Cavendish

1808-1891
William Cavendish
2nd Earl of Burlington (2nd creation)
7th Duke of Devonshire
Responsible for the layout and pews in the Priory Church. The Cavendish Memorial Fountain was built to commemorate his second son Lord Frederick who was assassinated in Phoenix Park, Dublin 12 hours after his arrival as Chief Secretary to Ireland in 1882.
≈
1812-1840
Lady Blanche Howard

1868-1938
Victor Cavendish
9th Duke of Devonshire
Enjoyed Grouse Shooting and entertained Edward VII and George V and Queen Mary at Bolton Hall.
≈
1870-1960
Lady Evelyn Fitzmaurice

1833-1908
Spencer Compton Cavendish
8th Duke of Devonshire
Provided a new water main to celebrate the Diamond Jubilee of Queen Victoria
≈
1832-1911
Countess Louise von Alten
"The Double Duchess"

The Cavendish Family Tree

Bolton Abbey Estate passed to The Cavendish family through the marriage of Lady Charlotte Boyle to William Cavendish, who became the 4th Duke of Devonshire in 1755.

Lady Charlotte's ancestors were the Lords of Skipton.

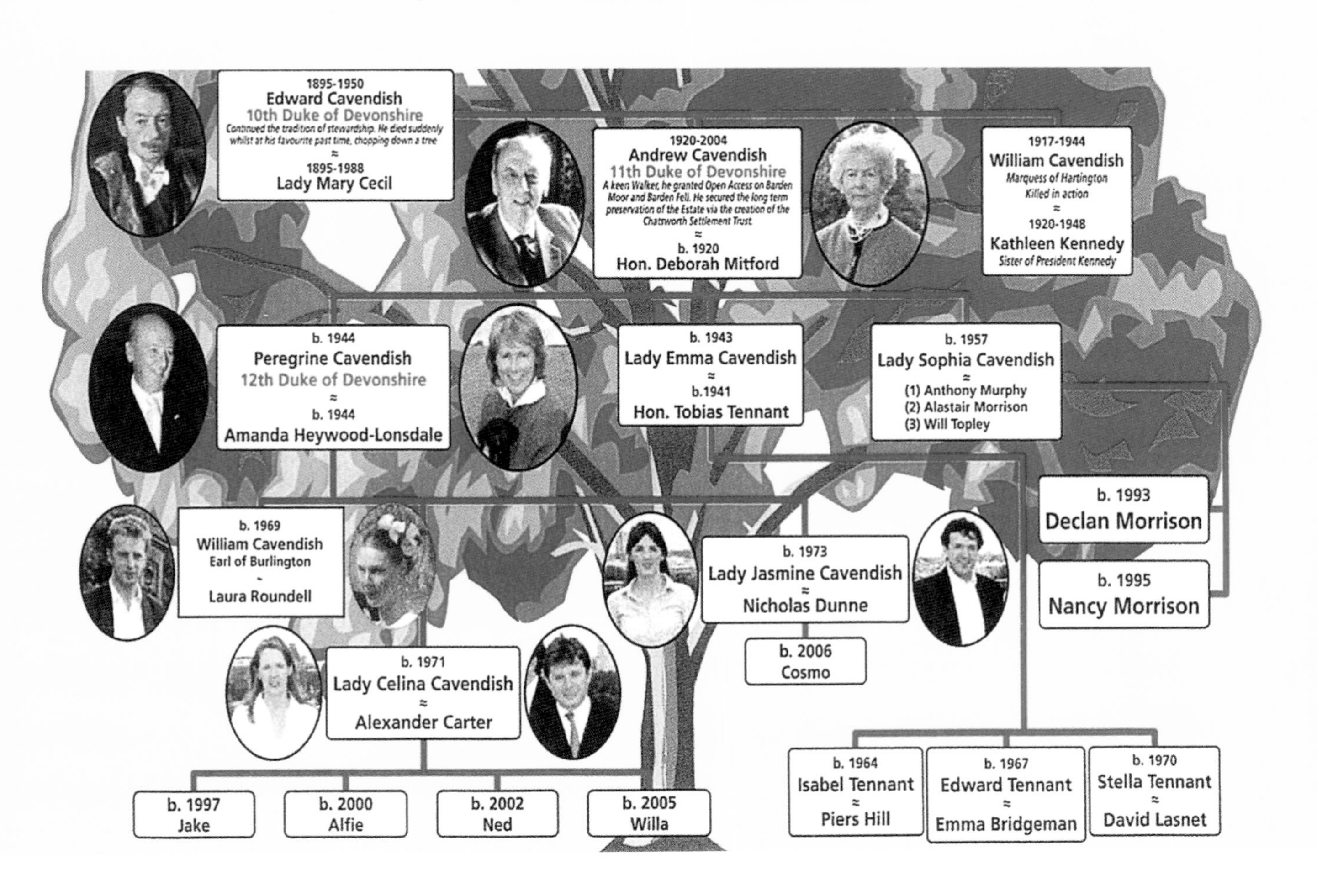

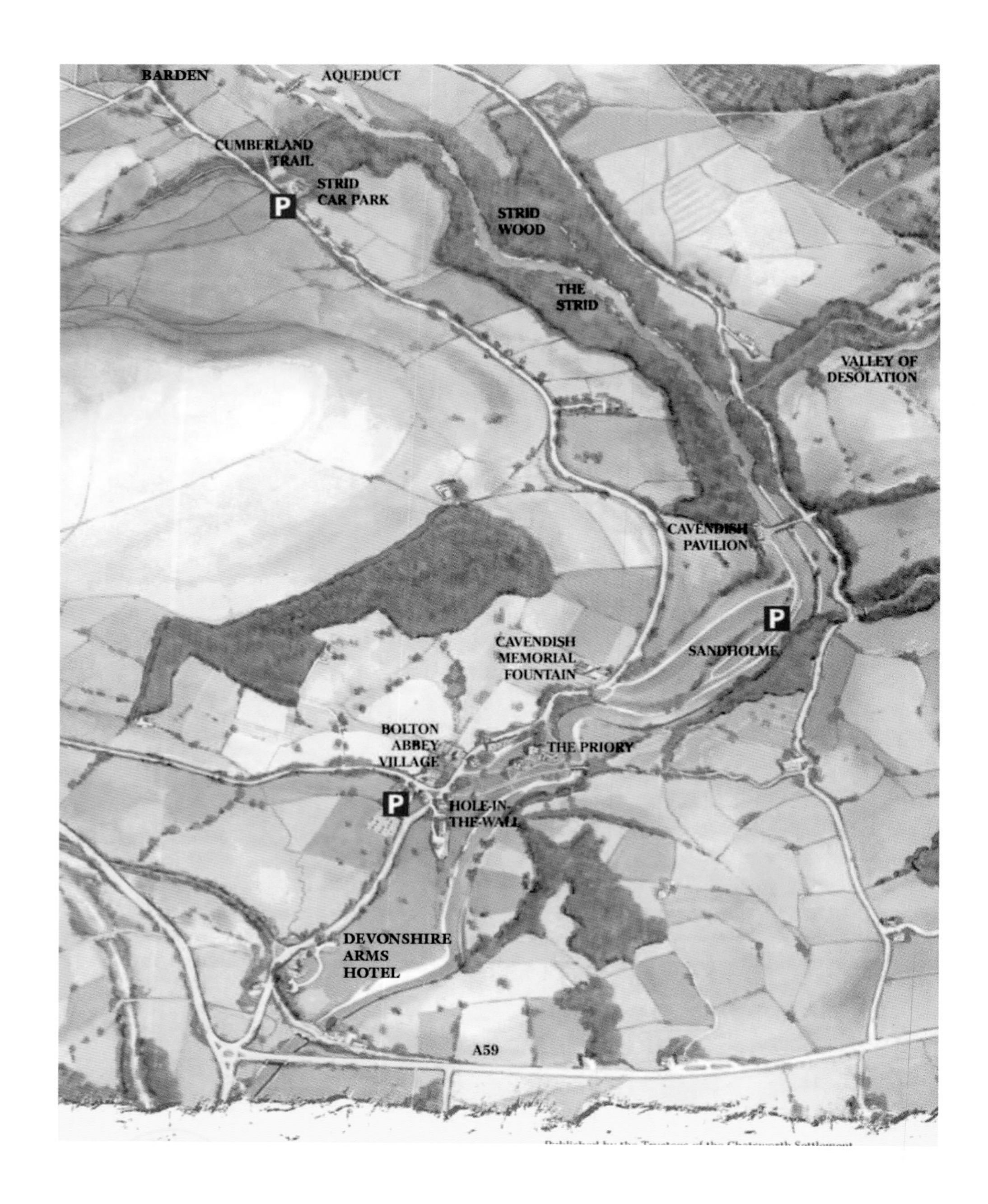

Map of part of the Bolton Abbey Estate in Wharfedale. Bolton Abbey to Barden

SUBSCRIBERS

A. F. Baines

Mrs. A. Crabtree

Jim Caygill

Colin Crabtree

Ian Farquhar

Bernard Foster

Leslie Gore

Grove Rare Books,
at Bolton Abbey

Laurence and Melissa Harwood

Mrs. S. Hersey

C. B. Harwood

T. H. Iveson

Ben Jones

Rosemary Murgatroyd

Major Simon Marriott

T. Muirhead

Ian R. Parsons

Mrs. D. R. Penrose

Nicholas Peto

Paul Robertshaw

J. Christopher Riddiough

Dr. and Mrs. P. I. W. Rowell

Colin Reeder

Michael A. Roberts

Colin Raw

Margaret Smith

Dr. P. H. W. Sheard

Michael H. Shaw

Paul Smeathers

Andrew and Janet Sharpe

Sedbergh School Foundation

Geraldine and Bob Starling

James and Karin Turnbull

R. B. Wardle

T. Peter Wall

Philip and Wendy Witten

Simon Ward

The Grosvenor Estate

James Pearson

Stephen C. Greenwood

D. J. Yorke

Peter Drew

Mrs. Valerie Ludlam

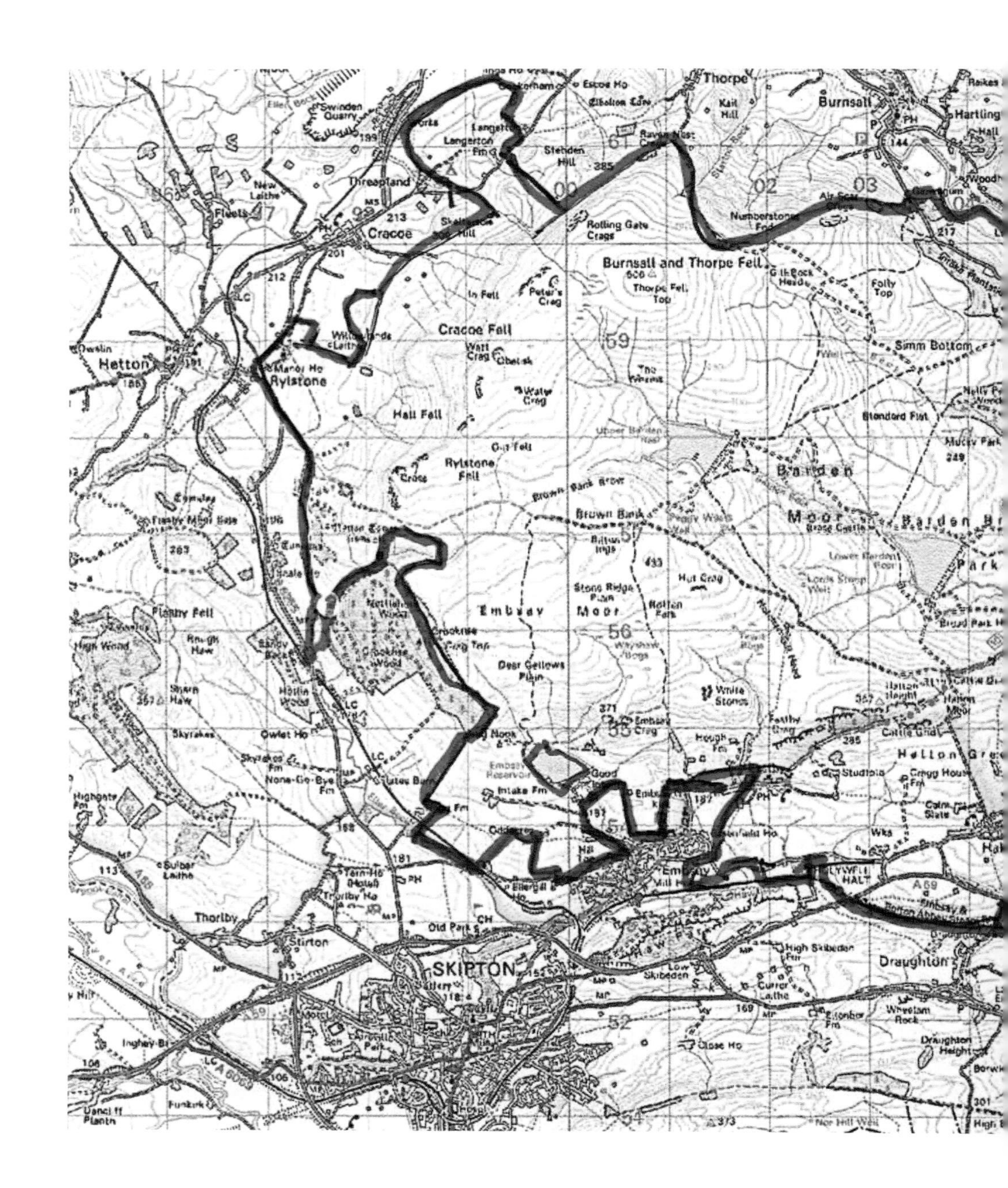
Thorpe
Burnsall
Swinden Quarry
Threapland
Cracoe
Rolling Gate Crags
Burnsall and Thorpe Fell
Thorpe Fell Top
Numberstones
Simm Bottom
Folly Top
Peter's Crag
Cracoe Fell
Hetton
Rylstone
Manor Ho
Hall Fell
Water Crag
Rylstone Fell
Brown Bank Brow
Brown Bank
Barden
Moor
Park
Lower Barden Resr
Stone Ridge Plain
Hut Crag
Embsay
Moor
Flasby Fell
Rough Haw
High Wood
Sharp Haw
Hetton
Hollin Wood
Skyrakes
Owlet Ho
Crookrise Wood
Deer Gallows Plain
White Stones
Embsay Crag
Embsay Reservoir
Intake Fm
Halton Height
Halton Moor
Cattle Grid
Studfold
Cragg House Fm
Draughton
None-Go-Bye Fm
Highgate Fm
Sulber Laithe
Thorlby
Stirton
Old Park
SKIPTON
Embsay
A59
A65
A6069
Low Skibeden
High Skibeden Fm
Wheelam Rock
Draughton Height
Funkirk
Close Ho

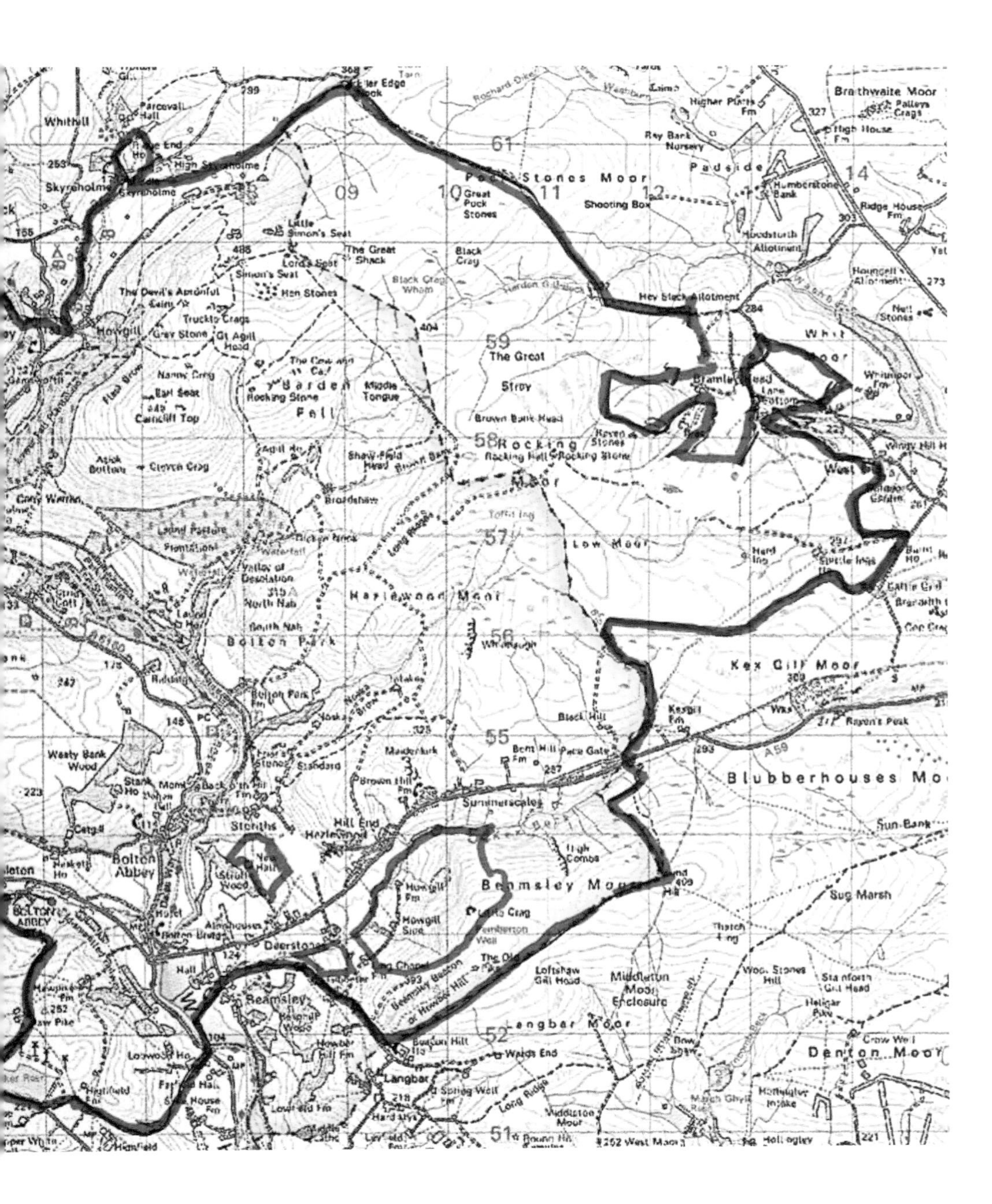
Braithwaite Moor
Whithill
Skyreholme
Parcevall Hall
High Skyreholme
Pock Stones Moor
Great Pock Stones
Shooting Box
Padside
Humberstone Bank
Ridge House Fm
Little Simon's Seat
Simon's Seat
Lord's Seat
The Great Stack
Black Crag
Hen Stones
The Devil's Apronful
Truckle Crags
Howgill
Grey Stone
Gt Agill Head
Hey Black Allotment
The Great Stray
Barden Fell
Rocking Stone
Middle Tongue
Nanny Crag
Earl Seat
Carncliff Top
Brown Bank Head
Rocking Moor
Raven Stones
Rocking Hall
Broadshaw
Low Moor
Hazlewood Moor
Valley of Desolation
North Nab
Bolton Park
Kex Gill Moor
Raven's Peak
Blubberhouses Moor
Black Hill
Kexgill Fm
Bolton Park Fm
Wharfedale
Pace Gate
Standard
Summerscales
Hill End
Hazlewood
Storiths
Bolton Abbey
Beamsley Moor
High Combs
Sun Bank
Sug Marsh
Thatch Ing
Middleton Moor Enclosure
Langbar Moor
Loftshaw Gill Head
Wood Stones Hill
Denton Moor
Beamsley
Langbar
Long Ridge
Middleton Moor
West Moor
Holling Hall
Crow Well
Low Wood Ho
A59

BIOGRAPHY OF J. M. SHEARD

John M Sheard was the Duke of Devonshire's right hand man who realised his ambition to work in the area he loved and grew up in.

Originally from Crosshills, near Skipton, he spent 33½ years working on the Bolton Abbey Estate and 28 years as its Senior Land Agent.

He has always loved the countryside and its environment in this part of Wharfedale and as a boy used to cycle there with friends and spend some hours by the river.

After being educated at Skipton's Ermysted's Grammar and Sedbergh schools he attended the Royal Agricultural College at Cirencester. He then worked for the Land Agents, Ingham and Yorke at Clitheroe for two years where he gained his qualification as a Chartered Land Agent and then was commissioned in the Royal Engineers for his National Service.

After that he gained valuable experience in land management working for Bidwells, the distinguished Land Agents in Cambridge. Three years spent with this firm stood him in good stead as his first application to the Bolton Abbey Estate secured him the job as deputy manager. Four years later he succeeded Ernest Hey as manager and he and his wife Brenda lived at the Beeches in Bolton Abbey village and then at the Old Rectory adjacent to the Priory.

Many awards have been forthcoming in the recognition of the Estate's services towards conservation, tourism, management and education. He is immensely proud of the trust put in him and the rest of the Estate workers by the Royal Family, and in particular, HRH the Prince of Wales, who visits occasionally knowing his desire for solitude, will be respected.

"I have seen the village develop into a thriving community. The Priory Church was moribund in 1966 but a new roof and other major renovations have seen it grow into a vibrant and lively place", he said, and due to his assistance with the Priory Church the Bishop of Bradford appointed him as an Honorary Lay Canon for five years.

In addition he has been chairman of the Bolton Abbey Parish Council for approximately 25 years, chairman of the governors of the Boyle and Petyt Primary School approximately 25 years, a member of the Country Landowners Association Yorkshire Committee for 5 years, a member of the Royal Forestry Society, and a member of various fishing committees, a life member of the National Trust and has enjoyed singing in the church choir, and is also a member of the Ilkley Choral Society and enjoys classical music. He is a long serving member of the Skipton Rotary Club and was awarded the Paul Harris Fellowship for outstanding service in 2002. He is a founder trustee of the Craven Trust, a local charity assisting communities in the Craven area. He thoroughly enjoyed taking part in village entertainment including annual concerts or pantomimes.

He is a countryman first and foremost, and on retirement looked forward to more "space", but due to the amazing variety of interests and valuable concerns of the owners he is sorry to finish working for the Duke of Devonshire on this Estate.

Red Grouse
by J. Bye